Also by Robert W. Fuller

Mathematics of Classical and Quantum Physics
(with Frederick W. Byron, Jr.)

Somebodies and Nobodies: Overcoming the Abuse of Rank

All Rise: Somebodies, Nobodies, and the Politics of Dignity

Dignity for All: How to Create a World Without Rankism
(with Pamela A. Gerloff)

RELIGION AND SCIENCE: A BEAUTIFUL FRIENDSHIP?

Robert W. Fuller

Copyright © 2012 by Robert W. Fuller

The symmetric design at the beginning of each
chapter was derived from a tile work in the
Alhambra palace in Granada, Spain.

The cover image incorporates a free wallpaper image of
the Andromeda Galaxy (M31) available for Mac OS X.

ISBN-13: 978-1479229024
ISBN-10: 1479229024

Author web site: www.robertworksfuller.com
Book web site: www.breakingranks.net
Huffington Post: www.huffingtonpost.com/robert-fuller

Printed in U.S.A

To my mother, Willmine Works Fuller,
who made me go to Sunday School,

and

my father, Calvin Souther Fuller,
who modeled the scientific method,

and

to my mentor, John Archibald Wheeler,
who accorded dignity to all.

Live your life as if there are no miracles
and everything is a miracle.
– Albert Einstein

Awe is an intuition of the dignity of all things, a realization
that things not only are what they are but also stand,
however remotely, for something supreme.
– Abraham Heschel

TABLE OF CONTENTS

PREFACE: REASON TO HOPE

[The 21st] century will be defined by a debate that will run through the remainder of its decades: religion versus science. Religion will lose.

    – John McLaughlin, TV talk show host[1]

Former priest John McLaughlin is hardly alone in his pessimism about religion's future. A spate of bestsellers— *The God Delusion*; *The End of Faith*; and *God Is Not Great: How Religion Poisons Everything*[2]—argues that religion, as we've known it, no longer serves the needs of people with a modern education and a global awareness.

Books like these have spelled out religion's shortcomings and I see no point in piling on. Rather, I will make the case that, in the long view, both religion and science come off as godsends (forgive the pun). And that, looking ahead, both are indispensable to letting go of old predatory practices and creating a fair, just, and peaceful world. If religion can see its way clear to making a mid-course correction and science can get off its high horse, John McLaughlin's prediction could be proven spectacularly wrong.

Many of the voices now being raised against religion are over-confident and patronizing, rather like those of trial lawyers who feel the jury is in their pocket. Perhaps that's because they are increasingly preaching to a public put off by science deniers, repulsed by clerical abuses, and alarmed by fundamentalist zealotry. Contemporary religious leaders, painfully aware of the relationship between public participation and institutional viability, know that religion is in a fight for its life.

I realize that this terrain is full of landmines. In the hope of defusing a few, let me acknowledge at the outset that the word religion means different things to different people. To some, it's knowledge and wisdom; to others, superstition and dogma. To some, it's worship; to others, wonder. To some, religion is salvation; to others, it's seeking. To some, religion is of divine origin; to others, it's manmade.

In this book, I'll use "religion" to refer loosely to the meta-physical, moral, and transformational precepts of the founders, prophets, saints, and sages of the major religions. The focus here is neither the theological doctrines associated with particular faiths nor the liturgical practices characteristic of various sects. Rather, the goal is to present a unifying perspective on the findings of religious and scientific inquiry.

Then, since the divergence between science and religion no longer serves either, I'll address the obstacles that have kept them from developing a "beautiful friendship" and describe the pay-off we may expect once they're on the same side.

Science gives us reason to think we can vanquish famine, disease, and poverty. Religion heralds "peace on Earth, goodwill toward men." Neither of these venerable institutions can deliver on its promise without help from the other, but together there is reason to hope that they can.

The book concludes with a model of morality that emerges, unexpectedly, as a peace dividend. As partners, science and religion can make the golden rule largely self-enforcing, and hasten our arrival into a world wherein everyone's dignity is secure.

I know this sounds utopian, but wait and see. Developments in both science and religion have created the possibility of a partnership. Ending centuries of fruitless squabbling and initiating a beautiful friendship is now possible.

I begin with what hooked me on these issues in the first place: the incompatible notions of truth advocated by my two schools: Sunday School and Public School.

Chapter 1: My Two Schools

My parents were not church-goers, but they thought their children should be exposed to the religious perspective. So, until we graduated from eighth grade, they made my brothers and me attend a Presbyterian Sunday School.

When I asked my Sunday School teacher how Jesus could turn a few fish and a little bread into enough food to feed a crowd, she explained it as a miracle. She gave the same answer about walking on water, raising Lazarus, and coming back from the dead. When I pressed her on the biblical account of creation—"He did all that in six days?"—she reread Genesis to the class.

My other school, a public school in Chatham, New Jersey, was located in the shadow of Bell Laboratories, where my father worked. Bell Labs was then one of the top scientific research labs in the world.

In third grade we studied the solar system. Our textbook had a diagram of Copernicus's heliocentric model showing the planets revolving around the sun in circles. A table gave the distance of each planet from the sun in miles and its period of revolution in days: 365 for the earth, 225 for Venus, just 88 for Mercury, and so on, all the way out to Pluto. Printed alongside each planet's orbit was its average speed in miles per hour as it circled the sun.

It was just then that we were studying circles in arithmetic. The lesson for the week was that the circumference of a circle

$C = 2\pi R$, where R is the circle's radius and π is a universal constant approximately equal to 3.14. A closeted nerd in the days before we had our own identity group, I decided to verify the speed shown for the orbiting earth using this formula. The computation was simple enough—just form the product $2\pi R$ and divide by the time—one year—that it took the Earth to complete one revolution.

But something was wrong. My result did not agree with the Earth's speed in the book. It was not even close. So I tried the same calculation for Venus and Mercury. No agreement with those either. I did the other six planets. Not one of my calculations agreed with the numbers in the book. Frustrated, I asked my father for help. He checked my figures, examined the textbook, and announced the unthinkable: *the book was wrong*. I had thought books couldn't be wrong. We all had.

The next day I showed the error to my teacher, Mrs. Bahoosian. It made her nervous. She drew me aside and spoke in a hushed voice. I think she worried that if word got out it might cast doubt on the entire educational enterprise among my peers. But she mollified me by promising to write the publishing company.

Months later she reported that the publisher was going to change the numbers in the next edition. She never told the class. I remember checking a year later and sure enough the errors had been corrected.

Catching that mistake broke the spell of the printed word, and a new notion of truth took hold of me: the truth is not necessarily what some authority says it is, but rather what can be proven.

But, if so, where did that leave the truths taught in my Sunday School? Some of what was taught there contradicted our science lessons. It seemed my two schools stood for two incompatible worlds: science and religion.

People hadn't always had to face this dilemma. For millennia, science and religion were not regarded as distinct. Religion offered explanations of life and the cosmos, and for a long time there was scant evidence to contradict them.

However, bit by bit, evidence contradicting the religious explanations was gathered and, by the seventeenth century, battle lines were forming. A more evidence-based way of pursuing truth was taking shape within the religious consensus, and sometimes the findings of those who insisted on seeing for themselves threatened the doctrine espoused by church leaders.

Science cited facts, made predictions, and tolerated dissent. In contrast, religion invoked scripture, urged faith, and required conformity. Science said, "Doubt me." Religion said, "Trust me."

As a child, I couldn't make peace between my Sunday School and my grade school, so I took the easy way out. I dismissed religion as unfounded and resolved to ignore it. With hardly a backward glance, I set my sights on a career in math and physics where I was encouraged to question authority.

But I did not go away empty-handed. I took with me a pair of questions that, in time, would shape my life's work.

Peace on Earth, Goodwill toward Men

It is not instruction but provocation that I can receive from another.

– Ralph Waldo Emerson

In Sunday School, I had noticed, everyone had noticed, that the commandments, precepts, and rules taught there were often disregarded, not only by the scoundrels and criminals we read about in the news, but by some of the very people whose job it was to teach us these morals.

Upon detecting hypocrisy in the messenger, my impulse had been to throw out the message. But I couldn't quite shake the golden rule. Its symmetry gave expression to an intuition that ran deep: that I shouldn't expect to be well-treated by those whom I treated poorly; that I should afford others the dignity I sought for myself.

My take-away questions from Sunday School were:

> **1.** Why are moral precepts—even those that everyone accepts—widely ignored?

> **2.** Why has "peace on Earth, goodwill toward men" not been realized?

I wondered about this gap between the ideal and the reality as World War II raged, as the Holocaust was revealed, and as Japan surrendered to American atom bombs. It seemed to me then, as it does now, that religion's most serious short-coming was not that it harbored "deniers" of well-established science models, but that it had not found a way to realize its own aspirational goals.

For example, the golden rule was suspended when it came to so-called "Negroes" (they were not allowed to own homes in my town), the mentally handicapped (a boy with Down Syndrome hung around my school's perimeter, but was barred from school property), homosexuals (a boy we thought "queer" was humiliated), and poor, overweight, unstylish, or "dumb" kids were often subjected to ridicule.

At college, when I argued that life might someday be created in a test tube, I was mocked as a "heathen" and dismissed as a "mechanist." When I responded with insults of my own, the result was a shouting match.

Later, I wondered if "getting even" gave me a pass when it came to obeying the golden rule. After all, *they* had hurled the first insult. But then, hadn't I upped the ante? The logician in me noticed that the golden rule, like the best rules in physics, allows for no exceptions. It didn't say anything about who went first. Did that mean that retaliating in kind—an eye for an eye, a tooth for a tooth—was wrong?

Finding an answer to this question took decades, and I'll return to it after addressing an even more fundamental, methodological question, a question that no discussion of religion and science can ignore.

Are There Really Two Kinds of Knowledge?

In the mid-1960s, stirred by the passions of the civil rights movement, I left physics to play a part in the reform of higher education then sweeping the country. Overnight, my life took an activist turn toward issues of equity and justice. Though exposure to the golden rule had predisposed me to sympathize with those demanding equal rights, I did not trace my political ideals to religion.

I'd spent most of my time since Sunday School in pursuit of scientific truth, where evidence rules. During that time, my skepticism toward the faith-based claims of religion had grown stronger. But in my political work, I couldn't help but notice that the reformers I worked with often invoked religious teachings to good effect in support of the goals we shared.

By the mid-seventies, the transformational energy of the sixties was spent and, seeing no chance for further reforms, at age thirty-seven, I left academia. The bitter academic politics of that period had left me bruised and burnt out. In search of a less contentious way to bring change, I wondered if the world's holy books contained anything that might have helped me be a better leader. In particular, Eastern religions, like Buddhism and Vedanta, were drawing attention from Western seekers, and the word was that they offered a more tranquil, enlightened path to personal and social change.

Before I could take in anything positive from religion, Eastern or Western, I had to deal with the negative. Yes, some churches had provided a home for leaders of the civil rights movement, but it seemed to me that if institutional religion practiced what it preached, it could have done a lot more to oppose racism and done it sooner. What more obvious violation of the golden rule could there be than segregation?

My old questions about religion's ineffectiveness were joined by new ones concerning its exceptionalism. What if religion defended its teachings in the same way science does—by marshaling evidence, making predictions, and testing them against outcomes? What if religion applied its teachings to its own practices? What if seemingly utopian prophecies like "peace on Earth, goodwill toward men"[3] were regarded not as naïve pieties but rather as testable *predictions* of a state of social equilibrium toward which humankind was groping?

It seemed to me that, with a few changes, religion could stand up to the criticisms of non-believers, regain the respect of its critics, and be the transformational force its founders and prophets had envisioned. In this re-visioning, the parts of religion that are counterfactual or unproven could either be dropped—as science jettisons theories that don't withstand scrutiny—or retained as speculation, metaphor, or personal preference. After all, anyone is free to believe anything, and most of us, including scientists, discreetly exercise that right in one area or another.

Fast forward thirty years. The twenty-first century has brought an avalanche of evidence, and official admissions, of religion's moral lapses. Extreme ideologues and fanatical true believers continue to tarnish the religious brand. When religion aligns itself with discredited science, its losing streak is unbroken, and in countries where educational levels are on the rise, religion is in decline. This wouldn't matter if religion had succeeded in imparting its most important teachings, but the golden rule is still widely flouted, and "peace on Earth, goodwill toward men" remains a distant dream.

Sometimes, when you can't get from A to B, it's for lack of a steppingstone. In that spirit, it seemed possible to me that for religion to realize its vision of peace on Earth, it may first need to make peace with science. The goal of this book is to show that religion and science can indeed co-occupy that steppingstone of peace, and from it, deliver on their complementary promises.

Although grievances leap to mind when we consider making peace with an old foe, ultimate success depends on identifying not where each side is wrong, but where each is right. Nowhere was this more evident than in ending the Cold War. One of the unacknowledged solvents of Soviet-American enmity was mutual acknowledgement by thousands of citizen diplomats of what each party to the conflict had got right. For example, that it was the Red Army that played the lead role in defeating the Germans in World War II; and that the USSR provided universal healthcare and access to affordable higher education to its citizens. Seeing some good in others doesn't mean blinding ourselves to what's wrong, and harping on the latter is no way to make peace with a foe.

Current attacks on religion are ignoring the fact that it got some very big things right. However, religion must take responsibility for much of the criticism directed its way because its spokesmen have repeatedly failed to distinguish between its great discoveries and its mistakes. Not only have some religious leaders ignored compelling evidence, but they, like the leaders of secular institutions, have all too often failed to live up to the standards of behavior they espouse. Nothing undermines authority like hypocrisy.

Paradoxically, science makes even more mistakes than religion; but it saves itself by being quicker to recognize and correct them. Niels Bohr, the father of atomic physics, ascribed his breakthroughs to "making my mistakes faster than others."

The difference between science and religion is not that one has "babies" in its bath water and the other doesn't. The difference is that science drains its dirty bath water faster, leaving its gleaming babies for all to admire. As the American scientific statesman, James B. Conant, said:

> The stumbling way in which even the ablest scientists in every generation have had to fight through thickets of erroneous observations, misleading generalizations, inadequate formulations, and unconscious prejudice is rarely appreciated by those who obtain their scientific knowledge from textbooks.

In what follows, I'll try to give both religion and science their due without soft-peddling their differences. Signing onto a new deal will require adjustments from both of these venerable antagonists.

The principal tool needed to end the historical enmity between science and religion, though nothing new, goes by a name that may be unfamiliar. It's called model building—"modeling," for short.

In ordinary language, models are representations of an object, a phenomenon, or a person or group that describe or prescribe the behavior of what's represented. Some models take the form of stories, rules, or codes that show us how to behave. Hence the phrase "*model* behavior." Other models take the form of explanations or theories that tell us how nature behaves, for example, Bohr's atomic *model*. These days one does not start a company without first creating a business *model*.

> *A model is a representation of an object, phenomenon, or person that resembles the real thing. By studying the model we can learn about what it mirrors.*

When we ask if there are two distinct kinds of knowledge—scientific truths and religious truths—we're really asking if the same methodology can unlock the secrets in both realms. The tool of modeling, coupled with demystification of the discovery process, provides a conceptual framework broad and deep enough to hold both science and religion.

I begin with a look at some models from science, then examine some models from religion. Once we have identified what's of lasting value—that is, some of the time-tested teachings—in both traditions, the next step is to spell out their complementary roles in addressing the life-threatening challenges facing humankind.

CHAPTER 2: SCIENCE

We Make Models

Man is a creature who makes pictures of himself, and then comes to resemble the picture.

    – Iris Murdock, as quoted by Simon Leys[4]

The title of Mark Twain's *What Is Man?* poses a question that humans have pondered for millennia. Our species modestly calls itself *Homo sapiens*—Man, the wise. We've also been dubbed Man, the builder; the tool maker; the game player; and the talker. Twain himself argued that man is a machine, *Homo machinus*.

While all these characterizations capture some aspect of humanness, none does so uniquely. On the contrary, it seems that every time someone makes a case that a particular trait sets humans apart, experts in animal life say, 'No, animals do that too.' Animals show intelligence and build nests, dams, and webs. They make tools, play games, and make war. They communicate and display emotion.

But no species other than ours holds the fate of the Earth in its hands. The question, then, is what is it about humans that has brought us such power?

There's one faculty that humans have developed more than other animals. It's our capacity to build ever more accurate and comprehensive models that explain the world and nature and thereby give us a measure of control over it. In this context, you can think of models as explanations and stories—explanations of how the world works; stories about how we ourselves behave.

I'm not saying that other animals don't employ models. Once again, the distinction doesn't appear to be absolute. We may never know when our hominid ancestors began inventing stories and telling fortunes, making maps and myths, keeping accounts and ledgers, depicting animals, explaining disasters, and speculating about death.

What's clear, though, is that these first steps to simulate aspects of the world and our place in it were taken at a time when there was no distinction between religion and science. Though we didn't think of it as modeling, building models was what we were doing. The crowning accomplishment of proto-religion and proto-science, which were then one, was the emergence of a model featuring us as individuals in the cosmos.

It's beside the point that these early models are now dismissed as "creation myths." What's important about them is not their validity but their existence. When humans began trying to explain the world, they embarked on a path that in time would give them a power advantage not only over other animals, but also over other human groups that handicapped themselves by clinging to inferior explanations.

Explanations, theories, maps, laws—models—are the path to power. Most of them are no good, but the few good ones rule. When models compete, better ones confer advantages on those who adopt them, and, over time, these first adopters gain an advantage over people saddled with models that harness and organize less power.

A Primer on Models

> *The sciences... make models. By a model is meant a ... construct which, with the addition of certain verbal interpretations, describes observed phenomena. The justification of such a construct is solely and precisely that it is expected to work.*
>
> – John von Neumann,
> creator of game theory and computer logic

Scientists use the terms "model," "theory," "explanation," and "law" almost interchangeably. The popular idea that a theory is more tentative than a model, or even a law, is quite wrong. These terms do not indicate relative degrees of certainty, but rather have their origins in history. For example, Newton's classical dynamics are referred to as "*laws* of motion" whereas the relativistic dynamics that Einstein discovered go by the name of the "*theory* of relativity." One might think the word law would indicate greater certainty, but in this case it's just the opposite. As of this writing, Einstein's "theory" has no known exceptions, and Newton's "laws" break down in the subatomic realm and for ordinary objects moving at high speeds.

Similarly, Darwin's "theory of evolution" is not so-named to suggest flaws in it. The theory of evolution has been thoroughly tested and to date has not been found wanting. Another very accurate, comprehensive scientific theory describes the elementary particles and their interactions. It goes by the unassuming name of "the standard model."

Building better models is humankind's defining activity. For better or worse, it's made us who we are. The aforesaid "standard model" describes three of Nature's four forces, and, by enabling us to predict their effects, allows us to tap sources of energy otherwise unavailable. The flip side of taming Nature's power is that we may use it in ways that damage the planet and harm each other.

We learn modeling early, starting with Legos, dolls, and model trains. The fables we grow up with can be understood as models that show us how to behave. People fancy themselves as characters in video games, sometimes deploying an avatar, and can try out different behaviors vicariously without risking their own lives.

Scientists Francis Crick and James Watson modeled the double-stranded helical structure of the DNA molecule with Tinker Toys. There is a model of the San Francisco Bay—complete with miniature piers poking into the water, a scaled-down Golden Gate Bridge, and "tidal currents" propelled by pumps—that fills a warehouse in Sausalito, California. By studying it, scientists can anticipate the effects of proposed real-world alterations of the Bay.

Weather bureaus, using computers and mathematical models, provide weather forecasts. As everyone knows, the predictions are not always right, but they're getting more accurate as the models are improved.

Experimenting with model planes in wind tunnels enabled the Wright brothers to build the aircraft they flew at Kitty Hawk. Even more significant than the plane they built was their pioneering use of modeling in engineering. Models enabled them to anticipate problems through trial and error without paying the price of crashing a piloted plane. Today, flight can be simulated on computers by representing both the airplane and the atmosphere in a mathematical model.

Grand unifying models are the holy grail of every branch of science. In biology, Darwin's theory of evolution by natural selection is such a model. In chemistry, it's Mendeleyev's periodic table of the elements. In geology, the theory of plate tectonics accounts for the earth's principal geological features. Physicists are searching for a "theory of everything" (often abbreviated TOE) that, as Leon Lederman, a Nobel laureate in physics,[5] picturesquely puts it, would "explain the entire universe in a single, simple formula that you can wear on your T-shirt." One of these models is called string theory.[6] Like all theories and models, string theory will ultimately live or die depending on whether its implications agree with observations.

Though much of science consists of building models, the use of models is hardly limited to science. Indeed, normative, prescriptive social models predate by millennia the descriptive and predictive nature models mentioned above. Beginning in the distant past, cultural codes of conduct—for example, the Ten Commandments—were used to regulate family and tribal relationships. Other examples of socio-political models include the theologies of religious institutions, organizational charts of universities, by-laws of corporations, and national constitutions.

Entrepreneurs and the venture capitalists who invest in their companies are guided by hypothetical plans—that is, models—that delineate scenarios based on various economic assumptions to chart a path to profitability. The governance models of nation-states range from the divine right of kings to fascism, communism, constitutional monarchies, and many sub-species of democracy. Sometimes users of social models actually lose sight of the difference between their models and reality. As Alan Greenspan, former Chairman of the Federal Reserve Bank, warns: "A surprising problem is that a number of economists are not able to distinguish between the models we construct and the real world."[7]

When we see parents, heroes, public figures, and fictional characters as "role models," we're using behavioral models to shape our own character.

In sum, models are descriptive or prescriptive representations of the world and ourselves. Their functions include providing us with an identity, shaping our behavior, maintaining social order, and guiding our use of power. Modeling has made humans what we are and our success as a species depends on learning to use them wisely.

Teen Epiphany: No Place to Stand

Know you what it is to be a child?
…it is to believe in belief.…

– Francis Thompson, 19th c. British poet

We don't forget our first ah-ha experience any more than we forget our first kiss. The difference is we have some idea of what to expect from a kiss, but we don't know what to make of an enlightening incident. The experience lingers in memory as something special, but since we can't account for it, we're apt to keep it to ourselves.

Only in my thirties did I realize that an experience I'd had in my teens was the analogue of that first kiss. About six years after discovering that our third grade science book contained mistakes, it struck me that *anything* could be wrong. There were no infallible truths, no ultimate explanations.

In high school we were learning that science theories and models were not to be regarded as absolute truths, but rather taken to be useful descriptions that might someday be replaced with better ones. I accepted this way of holding scientific truth—it didn't seem to undercut its usefulness. But I still wanted to believe there were absolute, moral truths, not mere assumptions, but unimpeachable, eternal verities. My mother certainly acted as if there were.

But one day, alone in my bedroom, I had the premonition that what was true of science applied to beliefs of every sort. I realized that, as in science, political, moral, or personal convictions could be questioned and might need amending or qualifying in certain circumstances. The feeling reminded me of consulting a dictionary and realizing that there are no final definitions, only cross references. I remember exactly where I was standing, and how it felt, when I discovered there was no place to stand, nothing to hold on to. I felt sobered, yet at the same time, strangely liberated. After all, if there were no absolutes, then there might be an escape from what often seemed to me to be a confining social conformity.

With this revelation, my hopes for definitive, immutable solutions to life's problems dimmed. I shared my experience of unbelief with no one at the time, knowing that I couldn't explain myself and fearing others' mockery. I decided that to function in society I would have to pretend to go along with the prevailing consensus—at least until I could come up with something better. For decades afterwards, without understanding why, I was drawn to people and ideas that expanded my premonition of a worldview grounded not on immutable beliefs, but rather on a process of continually improving our best working assumptions.

Science Models Evolve

It's the essence of models that they're works in progress. While nothing could be more obvious—after all, models are all just figments of our fallible imaginations—the idea that models can change, and should be expected to yield their place of privilege to better ones, has been surprisingly hard to impart.

Until relatively recently we seem to have preferred to stick to what we know—or think we know—no matter the consequences. Rather than judge for ourselves, we've been ready to defer to existing authority and subscribe to received "wisdom." Perhaps this is because of a premium put on not "upsetting the apple cart" during a period in human history when an upright apple cart was of more importance to group cohesiveness and survival than the fact that the cart was full of rotten apples.

Ironically, our principal heroes, saints and geniuses alike, have typically spilled a lot of apples. Very often they are people who have championed a truth that contradicts the official line.

A turning point in the history of human understanding came in the seventeenth century when one such figure, the English physician William Harvey, discovered that the blood circulates through the body. His plea—"I appeal to your own eyes as my witness and judge"—was revolutionary at a time when physicians looked not to their own experience but rather accepted on faith the Greek view that blood was made in the liver and consumed as fuel by the body. The idea that dogma be subordinated to the actual experience of the individual seemed audacious at the time.

Another milestone was the shift from the geocentric or Ptolemaic model (named after the first-century Egyptian astronomer Ptolemy) to the heliocentric model or Copernican model (after the sixteenth-century Polish astronomer Copernicus, who is regarded by many as the father of modern science).

Until five centuries ago, it was an article of faith that the sun, the stars, and the planets revolved around the earth, which lay motionless at the center of the universe. When the Italian scientist Galileo embraced the Copernican model, which held that the earth and other planets revolve around the sun, he was contradicting the teaching of the Church. This was considered sacrilegious and, under threat of torture, he was forced to recant. He spent the rest of his life under house arrest, making further astronomical discoveries and writing books for posterity. In 1992, Pope John Paul II acknowledged that the Roman Catholic

Church had erred in condemning Galileo for asserting that the Earth revolves around the Sun.

The Galileo affair was really an argument about whether models should be allowed to change without the Church's consent. Those in positions of authority often deem acceptance of their beliefs, and with that the acceptance of their role as arbiters of beliefs, to be more important than the potential benefits of moving on to a better model.[8]

Typically, new models do not render old ones useless, they simply circumscribe their domains of validity, unveiling and accounting for altogether new phenomena that lie beyond the scope of the old models. Thus, relativity and quantum theory do not render Newton's laws of motion obsolete. NASA has no need for the refinements of quantum or relativistic mechanics in calculating the flight paths of space vehicles. The accuracy afforded by Newton's laws suffices for its purposes.

Some think that truths that aren't absolute and immutable disqualify themselves as truths. But just because models change doesn't mean that anything goes. At any given time, what "goes" is precisely the most accurate model we've got. One simply has to be alert to the fact that our current model may be superseded by an even better one tomorrow.[9] It's precisely this built-in skepticism that gives science its power.

Most scientists are excited when they find a persistent discrepancy between their latest model and empirical data. They know that such deviations signal the existence of hitherto unknown realms in which new phenomena may be discovered. The presumption that nature models are infallible has been replaced with the humbling expectation that their common destiny is to be replaced by more comprehensive and accurate ones.[10]

Toward the end of the nineteenth century, many physicists believed they'd learned all there was to know about the workings of the universe. The consensus was that between

Newton's dynamics and Maxwell's electromagnetism we had everything covered. Prominent scientists solemnly announced the end of physics.

> *There is nothing new to be discovered in physics now. All that remains is more and more precise measurement.*
>
> – Lord Kelvin (1900)

Then a few tiny discrepancies between theory and experiment were noted and as scientists explored them, they came upon the previously hidden realm of atomic and relativistic physics, and with it technologies that have put their stamp on the twentieth century.

Albert Einstein believed that the final resting place of every theory is as a special case of a broader one. Indeed, he spent the last decades of his life searching for a unified theory that would have transcended the discoveries he made as a young man. The quest for such a grand unifying theory goes on.

CHAPTER 3: RELIGION

The most incomprehensible thing about the universe is that it is comprehensible.

    – Albert Einstein

God

With the idea of god, early humans were imagining someone or something who knows, who understands, who can explain things well enough to build them. Now then, if God knows, then maybe, just maybe, we can learn to do what He does. That is, we too can build models of how things work and use them for our purposes.

The idea of modeling emerges naturally from the idea of god because with the positing of a god we've made understanding itself something to which we can plausibly aspire. There has probably never been an idea so consequential as that of the world's comprehensibility. Even today's scientists marvel at the fact that, if we try hard enough, the universe seems intelligible. Not a few scientists share Nobel-laureate E. P. Wigner's perplexity regarding the *unreasonable* effectiveness of mathematics in the natural sciences.[11]

Comprehensibility does not necessarily mean that things accord with *common* sense. Quantum theory famously defies common sense, even to its creators. Richard Feynman is often quoted as saying, "If you think you understand quantum mechanics, you don't understand quantum mechanics." But a theory doesn't need to jibe with common sense to be useful. It suffices that it account for what we observe.

Our faith in the comprehensibility of the world around us mirrors our ancestors' faith in godlike beings to whom things were intelligible. Yes, it was perhaps a bit presumptuous of us to imagine ourselves stealing our gods' thunder, but *Homo sapiens* has never lacked for hubris.

Genesis says that after creating the universe, God created Man in his own image. The proverb "Like father, like son" then accounts for our emulating our creator, and growing up to be model builders like our father figure.

Just One God

In contrast to polytheism, where a plethora of gods may be at odds, monotheism carries with it the expectation that a single god, endowed with omniscience and omnipotence, is of one mind. To this day even non-believers, confounded by tough scientific problems, are apt to echo the biblical, "God works in mysterious ways."[12] But, miracle of miracles, not so mysterious as to prevent us from understanding the workings of the cosmos, or, as Stephen Hawking famously put it to "know the mind of God."

Monotheism is the theological counterpart of the scientist's belief in the ultimate reconcilability of apparently contradictory observations into one consistent framework. We cannot expect to know God's mind until, at the very least, we have eliminated inconsistencies in our observations and contradictions in our partial visions.

This means that the imprimatur of authority (e.g., the King or the Church or any number of pedigreed experts) is not enough to make a proposition true. Authorities who make pronouncements that overlook or suppress inconsistencies in the evidence do not, for long, retain their authority.

Monotheism is therefore not only a powerful constraint on the models we build, it is also a first step toward opening the quest for truth to outsiders and amateurs, who may see things differently than the establishment. Buried within the model of monotheism lies the democratic ideal of no favored status.

To the contemporary scientist this means that models must be free of both internal and external contradictions, and they must not depend on the vantage point of the observer. These are stringent conditions. Meeting them guides physicists as they seek to unify less comprehensive theories in a grand "theory of everything," or TOE. (A TOE is an especially powerful kind of model, and I'll say more about them later.)

There's another implication of monotheism that has often been overlooked in battles between religion and science. An omniscient, unique god, worthy of the designation, would insist that the truth is singular, and that it's His truth. In consequence, there cannot be two distinct, true, but contradictory bodies of knowledge. So, the idea of monotheism should stand as a refutation of claims that religious truths need not be consistent with the truths of science. Of course, some of our beliefs—be they from science or religion—will later be revealed as false. But that doesn't weaken monotheism's demand for consistency; it just prolongs the search for a model until we find one that meets the stringent condition of taking into account *all* the evidence.[13]

It is said that it takes ten years to get good at anything. Well, it's taken humans more like ten thousand years to get good at building models. For most of human history, our models lacked explanatory power. Models of that kind are often dismissed as myths. It's more fruitful to think of myths as early models, stepping stones to better ones. We now understand some things far better than our ancestors and other things not much better at all. But the overall trend is that we keep coming up with better explanations and, as more and more of us turn our attention to model building, our models are improving faster and our ability to usurp Nature's power is growing. To what purpose?

We'll discuss a variety of responses to this question later in the book. Religion famously heeds us to "separate the wheat from the chaff," and we'd be remiss if we did not apply this proverb to beliefs of every kind, including those of religion itself.

An Eye for an Eye

"An eye for an eye" comes down to us from King Hammurabi (18th century, BCE) who had it carved in stone at a time when there was no distinction between religion and science. It can be usefully understood not just as a formula for punishment, but rather as a simple descriptive model of how humans behave. When we're injured or abused, our immediate impulse is to do unto the perpetrator what's been done to us. We call it biblical justice. Often, victims of predation are not satisfied with merely getting even, but rather are inclined to "better the instruction," as Shylock points out in *The Merchant of Venice*. Escalation follows. Not to stand up to the perpetrator of a predatory act is to signal weakness and invite a follow-up that may bring death or enslavement.

It may be hard to tell who started a feud because the initial act of predation lies buried in a disputed past and escalation has since blurred the picture. A pattern of reciprocal indignities is what we see today in any number of ongoing conflicts around the world. At some point, it becomes more important to find a way to interrupt the cycle of revenge than to assign blame.

Attempts to stop cycles of predation by "turning the other cheek" can be suicidal unless they're part of a broad-based strategy of civil disobedience, and even then can result in great harm to protestors. Religious teachings, decoupled from political pressure, have seldom been enough to prevent predation or to arrest the cycles of vengeance that tend to ensue.

On the other hand, turning the other cheek, in the form of forgiveness—as institutionalized, for example, in "Truth and Reconciliation" commissions—is the only thing that can permanently end a cycle of revenge.

The Golden Rule

The golden rule embodies a symmetry reminiscent of those that turn up everywhere in physics models. A variant of the golden rule can be found in virtually every religion, ethical code, or moral philosophy.[14]

Do not do to others what would cause pain if done to you.
   – Hinduism

Treat not others in ways that you yourself would find hurtful.
   – Buddhism

What you do not want done to yourself, do not do to others.
   – Confucianism

What is hateful to you, do not do to your neighbor.
   – Judaism

Do unto others as you would have them do unto you.
   – Christianity

Not one of you truly believes until you wish for others what you wish for yourself.
   – Islam

We should behave to our friends, as we would wish our friends to behave to us.
   – Aristotle

Act only on that maxim through which you can at the same time will that it should become a universal law
   – Immanuel Kant's Categorical Imperative

Neminem laedere[15]
   – Legal codification of the golden rule, which
      translates as "general rule of care," or "hurt no one."

As in physics, a deviation from symmetry signals the existence of a force that breaks it. Among humans, asymmetries take the form of inequitable or preferential treatment of persons or groups and, as in the physical world, these deviations from the equal-handedness implicit in the golden rule reveal the existence of coercion. For example, slavery requires force or the threat of force.

If the most famous formula in physics is $E = mc^2$, then the golden rule, as a formula for reciprocal dignity, is perhaps its religious counterpart, a jewel in the crown of religious insight.

Dignity for All

If the idea of god, as signifying comprehensibility, were not enough to warrant a tip of the hat to religion, the god idea also contains the seeds of the egalitarian notion of universal dignity.

Notwithstanding the fact that religion has often impugned the dignity of adherents to other faiths, it has usually defended the dignity of its own followers. Theistic religions go further and proclaim the existence of a personal, caring god, a father figure who loves all who share the faith, according them equal dignity regardless of status, rank, or role.

The universal equality of dignity is among religion's most revolutionary ideas. It's not a description of life as we know it, but rather a prescription for life as it could be. Once formulated, the ideal of "dignity for all" exerts a pull that's felt in every human interaction. In the concluding chapter, I'll make the case that, despite appearances to the contrary, human behavior is slowly coming into alignment with that prophetic, aspirational, religious model.[16]

The need for dignity runs so deep that when our fellow man seems determined to deny it to us, even non-believers may suspend their disbelief. Arthur Hugh Clough gives this insight a comical twist:

> *And almost every one when age,*
> *Disease, or sorrows strike him,*
> *Inclines to think there is a God,*
> *Or something very like Him.*[17]

In the epigraph at the beginning of this book, Rabbi Abraham Heschel draws attention to dignity in an even larger sense. As we try to fathom our place in the cosmos, most of us, at one time or another, experience a sense of awe. Heschel interprets awe as an "intuition of the dignity of all things, a realization that things not only are what they are but also stand, however remotely, for something supreme."

The intuition of the dignity of all things is tantamount to recognizing that everything has an integral place in the whole, everything belongs and has an indispensable role. There is a perfection to things, not necessarily as they are at the moment, but rather at the next level up—as an inseparable part of the *process* of becoming. Everything is integral to the process, including our judgments and opinions, positive or negative, about what's happening. Heschel's observation recognizes this property of the universe and identifies awe as an appropriate response to the world's intricate integrity.

Again, it's now widely acknowledged that religion's record at upholding dignity is spotty. Religious leaders of every faith have at times sanctioned indignity toward others, persecuting them as infidels, heathens, and heretics.

Science makes as many mistakes as religion, probably more, but it rectifies them relatively quickly. As a result there are few who doubt its value. In contrast, the proposition that "The world would be better off without religion" has many takers.[18]

Religious models such as monotheism, the golden rule, and universal dignity are pillars of human civilization. Like science models, their strength is due to the truth they embody, and not dependent upon the zeal of "true believers." A prerequisite to realizing religion's vision of "peace on Earth, goodwill toward men" is a new relationship to the idea of belief itself.

Chapter 4: Belief

The public…demands certainties…But there are no certainties.

– H. L. Mencken

True Believers

When we hear the word fundamentalist, images of fanatical proselytizers, religious extremists, and suicide bombers leap to mind. But I shall use the word more broadly to refer to any true believers and even to that part of ourselves that might be closed-minded about one thing or another. By generalizing in this way, we include those who reflexively dismiss anything contrary to their own views, whether religious, scientific, artistic, or ideological. Such closed-mindedness is the antithesis of the modeling perspective.

Though the popular stereotype is that all fundamentalists are intolerant zealots, there are people who call themselves fundamentalists who hold that their beliefs are for themselves only, and who make no effort to convert anyone else. It may be that the fixity of their beliefs handicaps them—by keeping them ignorant of advances in scientific, political, or religious thought—but they're hardly alone in that regard.

Fundamentalism of the imperious sort comes in a variety of disguises: moral righteousness, technological arrogance, intellectual condescension, and artistic snobbery, to name a few. Such domineering forms of fundamentalism tend to be magisterial, overbearing, strident, elitist, and supercilious.

In a world without absolutes, fundamentalists' claims to represent higher authority would not be given special credence. In such a setting, inerrancy is out, fallibility is in. Questioning the current consensus is not only permitted, it's encouraged. The one thing that tolerance does not extend to is aggressive intolerance—that is, to coercive suppression of other points of view. Societies that do not protect freedom of speech and thought hamstring themselves and consign themselves to the backwaters of history.

Examples of fundamentalist close-mindedness include the traditional Confucianism that protects teachers in rural China against accusations of sexual abuse;[19] the Taliban's opposition to education for women and girls; the heedlessness of NASA officials who overruled the engineers on the doomed Challenger space shuttle mission; the "commissars" on the Nuclear Regulatory Commission who arbitrarily substituted their own judgment for that of hands-on operators at the near meltdown of the nuclear reactor at Three Mile Island; and, with catastrophic consequences, Japan's nuclear regulators who ignored warnings of the vulnerability of the Fukushima Daiichi Nuclear Power Plant to earthquakes and tsunamis.[20]

We all know that there are religious fundamentalists who would impose their beliefs on others and revile or excommunicate those who disagree with them. But, when scientists demean true believers they're indulging in one-upmanship not unlike that employed by the targets of their disdain. Religious fundamentalists, cocksure ideologues, crusading atheists, and smug scientists should not be surprised when derision and contempt for their opponents fail to change minds.

When adherents to any fundamentalist creed demonize dissenters as immoral or evil, they're treading a path that leads to dehumanization, oppression, and sometimes, in the extreme, to genocide. When nonbelievers derogate fundamentalists, they're taking a step down that same treacherous path.

> *If there is no God,*
> *Not everything is permitted to Man.*
> *He is still his brother's keeper*
> *And he is not permitted to sadden*
> *his brother,*
> *By saying that there is no God.*

> – Czeslaw Milosz, Nobel-laureate in Literature

To Use Beliefs or Be Used by Them? *That* Is the Question.

> *Modern art writ large presents one cultural expression*
> *of a larger political gamble on the human possibility of*
> *living in change and without absolutes.*

> – Kirk Varnedoe, museum curator

Living without absolutes takes some getting used to. It requires breaking our dependency on "intoxicating certitudes,"[21] resisting the temptation to stifle debate by invoking authority, and, instead, marshaling the evidence for the best models we've got.

When our models can't change, behavior patterns become frozen, and some of them are apt to be abusive and unjust. The peace and prosperity of the world depend on attitudes about the evolution of models and our degree of comfort in allowing this process to unfold.

One reason it can be so hard to accept the notion of changing models is that they are composed of interlocking sets of fondly held beliefs. Nothing dies harder than one's own cherished opinions. Many people are so identified with their beliefs that they react to the idea of revising them as they would to the prospect of losing an arm or a leg. Institutions are usually even more resistant to change.

Avoiding the violence this breeds requires that we learn to hold our beliefs not as immutable absolutes but rather as working assumptions which, taken together, function as a pragmatic model. As we've seen, this is how scientists are taught to hold their theories. Adopting this posture is equally important to artists, chefs, dancers, or anyone seeking to develop their craft. Indeed, it is how people who are really good at what they do conduct themselves before going public with their finished product. Typically, a great deal of prior improvisation and experimentation occurs behind the scenes.

Creative people in every line of endeavor adopt beliefs provisionally for their usefulness and elegance and consider new ones with open minds to see if they are improvements over those they currently hold. They hold beliefs not unto death, but until they find more accurate, comprehensive, useful replacements that prove their worth by leading to more precise predictions, better pies, or more beautiful dances or paintings. Welcome to the post-fundamentalist era!

Detachment from our beliefs does not imply indifference, let alone resignation. The instinct to defend our beliefs serves a higher purpose. Usually disagreements have a legitimate basis and the only way to advance toward a reconciling model is to advocate for our views as effectively as we can while others do the same for theirs. We fail to serve the search for an improved model if we don't mount the strongest possible defense of our present ideas. Each of us helps discover the new model by holding out until our individual perspective can be absorbed into a broader public synthesis stripped of personal idiosyncrasies.

The duty to defend our beliefs to the best of our ability is one of the main themes in the Hindu holy book, *The Bhagavad Gita*. In a key passage, Lord Krishna counsels Prince Arjuna to do battle with his foes—even though they include relatives and former allies—impersonally, dispassionately, and unreservedly.[22] The adversarial method, while intense, need not be personally antagonistic, even in those especially awkward situations in which we know our opponents intimately. Once we accept the inherent fallibility of beliefs, it's easier to allow for ideas that differ from our own. From there, it's but a small step to recognizing the individuals who hold opposing views as valid interlocutors, undeserving of contempt.

If, in the end, it's our own case that crumbles, we can simply admit our error without loss of face and join in welcoming the discovery of something new and better. When our beliefs go to battle and lose, we ourselves live to argue another day, just as lawyers do when a judgment goes against one of their clients. Though all models eventually come up short that doesn't mean that, in the interim, some models are not more useful than others. The alternative to fundamentalism is not relativism, it's model building.

Not infrequently we sense our own mistakes at about the same time others do. Why is it so difficult to acknowledge errors publicly? It's because we fear that admitting to imperfection will expose us to indignity, if not outright rejection.

But, the most successful modelers have usually found ways to admit their errors—at least to themselves—and move on. Niels Bohr prided himself on making his mistakes faster than others. He also held that the opposite of any deep truth is also a deep truth, and would routinely invite people to imagine the opposite of their own pet theories and beliefs. And, after they'd done that, then to imagine the opposite of the opposite, which need not necessarily return them to their starting point.

People capable of handling political differences, artistic ambiguities, personal disagreements, scientific discrepancies, philosophical paradoxes, and identity crises are the opposite of ideologues. They must cultivate an equanimity and detachment, and let go of personal preferences, self-righteousness, and blame. Mature modelers are problem-solvers or artists in search of a synthesis that satisfies all parties or, after internalization, the contrary voices sounding in their own heads.

> *Each person has a piece of the truth, but no one has the whole of it. The first step to a broader truth is to take a stand strongly for our own piece of it, and then to engage in principled struggle with those who disagree. If we listen, more truth emerges from the struggle.*
>
> – paraphrase of Gandhi's truth-seeking strategy[23]

Learning to see science models as provisional has resulted in previously unimaginable technological and economic gains. *A parallel transformation in which we open ourselves to modifications of our personal beliefs will do likewise for global peace, social harmony, political partnership, and personal development.*

Models have the extraordinary property of shielding the dignity of individuals who espouse them. You can champion a model that turns out to be wrong, but that does not make *you* less worthy.

Moreover, models aim to reconcile all points of view, to account for everyone's perceptions, and to validate everyone's experience. In short, a good model is a synthesis (not a compromise) that makes everyone right in at least some respect. Needless to say, when no one feels a loss of face, when everyone's dignity survives a conflict, the chances of the various parties working together in the aftermath are much improved.

While there's no denying that we need working beliefs, we can get along quite nicely without absolutes. We need only resist elevating beliefs into eternal verities. To know who we are does not mean we know who we'll become.

Although Bohr and Einstein disagreed on quantum theory, their dialogue is as exemplary for its respectfulness as it is famous for delineating a divide in the road of human thought. The jury is still out on the substance of their disagreement.

Moral codes are prescriptive behavioral models and, like all models, they evolve. This does not mean they're arbitrary or even "relativist" in the sense that "anything goes." That morals lack universality and infallibility does not mean we are free to ignore them where they do apply—just as the inapplicability of Newtonian mechanics in the atomic realm does not render Newton's laws inapplicable to planets and projectiles. On the contrary, in its applicable domain a particular principle—scientific or moral—will remain as valid as ever. Making such distinctions is part of learning to live without certainty, to inhabit a post-fundamentalist world.

The truth is we've been living without absolutes from the start. There really never were any, but until now we've needed to believe in them much as children fix on certain beliefs while they get their bearings. With adolescence, we temper these beliefs, and with maturity we can let go of belief in belief itself.

In the realm beyond belief, everything looks a bit different. That's why I was thrown off balance when I stumbled upon this terrain as a teen in my bedroom. At first you feel unmoored; then you smell freedom. Not freedom to do anything, but enough freedom from conventional wisdom to question dogma and loosen its shackles, if not escape its confines.

As we come to see ourselves as separate from, and senior to, our beliefs, we realize that we'll survive a change in them. They're our servants, not our master.

It is on the neutral ground beyond belief that science and religion can meet, do meet, and in truth have always met, protestations of the authorities notwithstanding. On this common ground, where evidence is king—and where, if the evidence itself is in dispute, the appeal is to evidence about evidence rather than to dogma—science and religion can build a beautiful friendship.

CHAPTER 5: MYSTERY

The most beautiful thing we can experience is the mysterious. It is the source of all true art and science.

– Albert Einstein

While it's true that science aims to explain and, in that sense, demystify, there remains something ineffable about the *process* of discovery. I've mentioned the perplexing fact that nature is understandable, not just in broad outline, but in fine detail. It strikes many as mysterious that nature has spawned a creature—*Homo sapiens*—who comprehends her well enough to steal her power.

A further mystery attaches to quests of every sort—scientific, artistic, and spiritual. The deep similarities between the eureka of science, the epiphanies of art, and the revelations and enlightenment of religion provide a bridge that helps close the gap between the two vocations.

Eureka, Epiphany, Revelation, Enlightenment

Description demands intense observation, so intense that the veil of everyday habit falls away and what we paid no attention to, because it struck us as so ordinary, is revealed as miraculous.

– Czeslaw Milosz

Scientific research culminates in the "eureka" of discovery. Artists describe their creative breakthroughs in remarkably similar language. Political transformation often originates in the discovery of a new personal identity, which then forms the basis of a revised group consensus. (As the modern women's movement taught us, "the personal is political.") Religious practices aim variously for revelation, illumination, self-realization, union with God, or enlightenment.[24]

In each of these realms, protracted immersion in mundane details can lead to epiphanies. They may feel like bolts from the blue, but they are usually preceded by months, years, or even decades of painstaking investigation. For what seems an eternity, we go up one blind alley after another, experience failure upon failure. Without this preparatory groundwork, breakthroughs almost never occur. It is only when we're steeped in a subject—often feeling confused and hopeless—and are on familiar terms with the contradictions that characterize the field, that resolution may occur. Breakthrough takes the form of a revelatory insight wherein an old, collapsing model is superseded by one that removes some, if not all, of the contradictions. Depending on the realm, "better" can mean more useful, effective, accurate, comprehensive, simple, beautiful, elegant, or loving. Convincing others that what we've come upon is indeed better may take longer still, sometimes beyond our lifetime.

Some breakthroughs get the Nobel Prize, some an acknowledging nod from a companion or a stranger. Other epiphanies are met only with inner recognition. But all bear the stamp of a habit broken and provide us with a new way of beholding the world or ourselves.

From this perspective, the experience of enlightenment—whether in a scientific, artistic, political, or religious context—is seen as a movement of mind that lasts but an instant rather than as a sublime state which, once attained, becomes permanent. In the framework of modeling, enlightenment is the exhilarating experience of a fresh perception breaking the stranglehold of the habitual. In Milosz's phrase, what has seemed ordinary is "revealed as miraculous." The differences in enlightenment from one field to another pale in comparison with the deep similarities common to enlightenment in every realm—a sense of blinders removed, of clear-sightedness, of ecstatic revelation.

The experience of enlightenment can be thought of as a leap across a precipice from one foothold to another. For a while after landing we may feel elated, but it's a mistake to confuse this afterglow with enlightenment. Enlightenment is not the condition into which we have vaulted; it's the leap that took us there.

That moments of enlightenment can't be anticipated accounts for part of our fascination with them, but it also makes the experience vulnerable to mystification. History has seen many claimants to the titles of sage, genius, maestro, saint, or enlightened master. Mesmerized by the aura of celebrity and mystery that envelops them, we often fail to notice that, like ourselves, they are human beings. When they're not having an epiphany—which is most of the time—they're ordinary in the same way that everyone is. What sets some of them apart is a readier ability to rise above habit and see freshly. And sometimes they can transmit this special skill to their students. Whether using it will result in a student hitting the jackpot, or, for that matter, in the teacher hitting a second jackpot, or either of them ever having another enlightening experience—of that there are no guarantees.

Students and seekers often collude in their own infantilization by maintaining habits of deference that lull them into believing that an experience of enlightenment is quite beyond them. Such dependent relationships with revered authority figures reflect the escapist desire for a parent whose love is constant, whose wisdom is infallible, and on whom we can always rely. The best teachers, like the best parents, freely transmit their knowledge, skills, and passion for truth-seeking to their mentees, but without leaving them starry-eyed. As with so many of the most precious gifts in life, the best we can do to repay such benefactors is to pass what we've learned from them on to someone else.

In religious traditions, teachers impart the deepest truths to their students through what is aptly called "transmission of mind." These truths are often actually meta-truths, that is, they're insights into the truth-seeking process itself. The notion of "transmission" expresses the transfer of modeling skills regardless of the field of inquiry. There were times during my physics training when I felt I was experiencing a transmission of mind from my mentor, Professor John A. Wheeler, merely by hanging out with him and observing him closely as he tackled problems. Sometimes he'd pass on something he attributed to his mentor, Niels Bohr. Transmitters of mind are invariably part of a lengthy lineage consisting of parents, grandparents and teachers.

When it comes to the discovery process, the differences between the eurekas of science and the revelations of religion are superficial. Yes, scientists wear lab coats and jeans, and we imagine prophets in tunics and loincloths, but investigators of every kind base their insights on meticulous observation and treasure the rare "ah-ha" moments. The similarity of the *process* whereby new truths are found, whether in science or religion, strengthens the case for letting go of the ancient antagonism that has bedeviled their relationship and embarking on a beautiful friendship.

Ah-ha and Ho-hum

In the aftermath of movement politics, California was teeming with seekers after truth. More than a few political activists had replaced their concerns about social justice with a quest for personal enlightenment. I was skeptical but intrigued by rumors of a state of consciousness promising clarity of mind and perception.

I knew a number of high achievers in mathematics, physics, politics, and the arts, and I wanted to know if attaining enlightenment would be helpful in such fields. If enlightenment is indeed a state of exceptional lucidity, it ought to affect the quality of the work done by those who've attained it.

To check this out, I read widely and attended talks, seminars, workshops, and retreats with dozens of teachers and gurus representing a variety of spiritual traditions.[25] I got to know several gurus personally, as well as some of their advanced students privy to what went on behind the curtain separating the novices from the gurus. How did these presumably enlightened masters act when they were not functioning in their role as spiritual leaders in front of a group of devoted followers?

Getting a close look at several individuals who were advertised as enlightened led me to conclude that there's a lot of hype and hypocrisy in the business. A good many of them, not unlike a fair number of academics I'd known, seemed to me to be in it primarily for the lifestyle.

Many gurus are treated like deities and hold absolute power over their devotees. As "enlightened beings" they're accountable to no one, and their foibles, appetites, and excesses are given a pass. Of course, there were some teachers who, as far as I could make out, lived exemplary lives. But lack of transparency and accountability ensnare leaders of all types in corruption, and spiritual leaders are no exception.

Fraud is a stranger to neither science nor religion. Its presence invalidates neither, but its ubiquity warrants skepticism. What I really wanted to find out was whether there were claimants to enlightenment who, unlike ordinary people, actually pass their days in a state of bliss and clarity. And, if attained, does enlightenment persist? Are the enlightened more creative *subsequent* to attaining *satori*, to use the Zen term for enlightenment? Are they kinder, wiser, or more creative than the unenlightened?

None of the teachers I asked gave unequivocal answers to these questions. Nor did any of them unambiguously exemplify the supposed benefits of enlightenment. Many identified with traditional religious rituals or techniques, and saw their job as grafting these onto contemporary American culture. The language of enlightenment tended to be esoteric, obscurantist, and elitist, and the teachings attracted more credulous dilettantes than credible seekers.

In the end, I concluded that while certain people do attain an unusual degree of insight into the workings of the mind, their default consciousness did not seem different in kind from that of other extraordinary individuals who made no claim to enlightenment and indeed were skeptical about the idea.

During quiet moments, when our current identity is withdrawn, "off duty" as it were, we can see ourselves as nothing special no matter how grand our public persona, or nothing shameful no matter how lowly our social status. We just are what we are, unburdened of opinions, free of judgment and guilt, released from striving, perhaps inclined toward empathy, perhaps not. We take things in, and we witness ourselves doing so. We see the world whole and are not separate from what we behold. We may experience euphoria, or just tranquility.

Regardless, neither euphoria nor tranquility lasts. Presently, when the world calls us back to the ho-hum of everyday life, we have to assume a working identity because not to have one is to have no way to participate in the life game. Even gurus who style themselves as having no identity are assuming the identity of someone who fancies himself or herself to be egoless.

I've come to think that the eradication of the ego is no more workable than doing without the other pillar of being—the body. Rather than downgrading either, it's better to give them both their due by maintaining them in good working order.

In my quest, I did not come across anyone who could be said to *dwell* in a state of permanent enlightenment. No doubt, some experienced bliss, but, as far as I could tell, it was intermittent.

The term enlightenment is sometimes used to denote the *knowledge* of the insubstantiality and malleability of identity and sometimes to refer to an *experience* of the insubstantiality of self. Knowledge may last, but an experience can't be bottled. In this regard, enlightenment is like happiness: treasured all the more for its intermittence.

Enlightenment practices, not unlike mathematics and physics, are often obfuscated. A few centuries ago, reading and writing were such rare skills that possessing them set people apart. In the same way that literacy has spread, so too will people everywhere become conversant with experiences of enlightenment, recognizing them as the unmoored feeling of pivoting from an old model (which may range from a single belief to a personal identity) to a new one.

The Miraculous

The miracle is not to walk on water, but to walk on earth.

– Thich Nhat Hanh

The allure of mystery points directly to the nature of reality as open and infinite. It offers a foretaste of our real power within that reality as its discoverer and knower.

But because of its connection with power, the miraculous seduces some into magical thinking. Both the fraudulent and the profound appear at first to violate our expectations. Science has learned to examine puzzling new phenomena from all angles to see if there isn't a way of accounting for them from known principles. New evidence may force scientists to revise their best, most comprehensive theories, but only as a last resort. This essential feature of science is captured in an oxymoronic description that scientists sometimes apply to their methodology—*radical conservatism.*

The appeal of the mysterious has its origin in our desire to free ourselves from any "box" in which we find ourselves. Our vicarious delight in the escape artist's success is an expression of our will to freedom.

But our true powers lie closer to hand, and may be tapped to the extent that we understand how Nature works. Miracles do not consist of violations of Nature's laws but rather of aligning ourselves with them with such fidelity that we partake of her miraculous powers.

Hearts and Minds

Despite some egregious moral lapses and its losing streak when it aligns itself with discredited science, religion still holds a special place in the hearts of many. This is partly attributable to its genius for multitasking. Religion consoles and guides. It commends and condemns. It awes and humbles. It helps believers to endure the unendurable.

One need not belong to a particular faith to see that shared religious beliefs promote social cohesion which in turn facilitates cooperation. A group's ability to respond to natural or manmade catastrophes depends on nothing so much as unity. As Lincoln, quoting Jesus, noted, "A house divided against itself can not stand." Shared religious beliefs can hold a house together.

On the personal front, religion helps to take us out of ourselves so—as *witnesses* to our own behavior—we can see how we're affecting others and make adjustments. Above all, religion affirms human dignity and helps us cope with the indignities and losses that invariably befall us.

When it comes to personal transformation, religion has not only made fundamental contributions in its own right, but has also inspired great art and literature. Classics by Dante, Cervantes, Shakespeare, Milton, Goethe, Melville, Balzac, Dostoevsky, Hugo, and others serve as handmaidens to the world's holy books.[26]

Examples of religious insight into personal change can be found in all the religious traditions, but I'll cite only two, drawn from Christianity and Hinduism, respectively—the doctrines of resurrection and reincarnation. As applied to the physical body, these tenets are arguable. Nonbelievers reject them outright and even many believers take them metaphorically. That some people do take such doctrines literally does no harm to those who do not, and since evidence is hard to come by, this is a realm where agreeing to disagree is not an inexcusable cop out.

Interpreted metaphorically, however, and applied to modeling, these ideas are arguably profound. Models must "die to be reborn," none more dramatically than our self models or identities. The disintegration of a current identity is often experienced as a kind of death. The struggle to come to terms with the loss of a partner or child, or with a sudden change in our status or health, can feel like what St. John of the Cross described as a "dark night of the soul."

From the modeling perspective, resurrection and reincarnation can be understood not as migrations of the soul, but rather as metamorphoses of the *identity*. In today's rapidly changing world, most of us experience several distinct changes of identity. Yes, the process occurs *within* one's lifetime rather than connecting one life span to another as some theologies suggest. Many find reassurance for life's most hazardous passages in the Bible, the Talmud, the Koran, the Upanishads, and Sutras. That the core teachings in these books serve many as illuminating and consoling guides to self-transformation is why they're deemed holy.

During those perilous passages where one identity dissolves and another crystallizes in its place, we are at maximum vulnerability, like a crab molting its shell. When a familiar identity disintegrates, we may doubt our worth. At times the community we normally depend on for support, even the fellowship of friends and family, can fail us, and we may find ourselves defenseless and alone.

Religion serves when it illuminates the process through which we morph from one identity to another. Religion combines art, literature, and theater in the context of communal fellowship to effectively transmit truths about the identity and its transformation that help people maintain their balance in a world in flux. The future of vocations that can help us through the whitewater of traumatic change is secure.

Foundation for a Beautiful Friendship

The preceding chapters provide a basis for rapprochement between religion and science. The dysfunctional relationship that now exists between them could be retired in favor of a beautiful friendship if they would acknowledge that:

◆ Both religion and science make use of educated guesses to identify new truth, devise rules, construct theories, and build models.

◆ Religious and scientific models that are found wanting must be revised or discarded.

- Human fallibility means revisions are the rule, not the exception. We're well advised to "try, try again," because one success, which may then spread via imitation, makes up for countless failures.

- Both religious and scientific precepts must be grounded in painstaking observation and are defended by reference to such evidence.

- The *act* of discovery—though it goes by the different names of eureka, epiphany, revelation, and enlightenment—is basically the same in all fields. An occasional ah-ha punctuates a lot of ho-hum.

- Religion and science reduce suffering in complementary ways: science by alleviating material wants and curing disease; religion by cultivating kindness and compassion.

- Both religious leaders and scientists have sometimes put their institutional interests above the public interest. Both religion and science have also produced leaders who have sacrificed themselves for truth, beauty, and justice.

Science gives us reason to think that hunger, disease, and scarcity can be overcome. Religion harbors the hope that peace is attainable. In the remaining chapters, I'll try to show how, together, religion and science could deliver on the dual dream of sufficiency and decency.

CHAPTER 6: PEACE BETWEEN SCIENCE AND RELIGION

Moral Models Evolve, Too

When religion has committed itself to a particular science model, it has often been left behind as the public embraced a new model. That's the position in which the Catholic Church found itself in defending Ptolemy's geocentric model of the solar system against the simpler heliocentric model of Copernicus. It's the situation in which supporters of "creationism"—and its offspring, "intelligent design"—find themselves today.

Many contemporary religious leaders do not make this mistake, although those who do get a disproportionate amount of attention. Religious leaders who cheerfully cede the business of modeling nature to science are no longer rare. Neither they nor the scientists who study these matters, many of whom are themselves people of faith, see any contradiction between the perennial wisdom embodied in the world's religions and, say, Darwin's theory of evolution, the geological theory of plate tectonics, or the Big Bang theory of the cosmos.

It may surprise some that the father of modern cosmology, George Lemaître, was a priest.[27] When asked how he reconciled his faith and his science, he wrote:

> *The writers of the Bible were ... as wise or as ignorant as their generation. Hence it is utterly unimportant that errors of historic or scientific fact should be found in the Bible....*[28]

Father Lemaître showed that Einstein's general relativity predicted an expanding universe. Einstein, convinced that the universe was static, modified his theory to avoid this implication. Later, when the universe was found to be expanding as Lemaître had predicted, Einstein withdrew the modification, declaring it the biggest blunder of his life.

Tenzin Gyatso, the Dalai Lama, put it unequivocally in an op-ed in *The New York Times*, "If science proves some belief of Buddhism wrong, then Buddhism will have to change."[29]

That any of the currently accepted scientific theories could, in principle, be incorrect or incomplete is taken for granted by the scientific world. To insist, for example, that the theory of evolution is "just a theory" is only to state what every scientist knows and accepts. Of course, it's a theory. What else could it be? But it's an extremely well-tested theory and it makes sense to use it unless and until we have something manifestly superior. A society that rejects the theory of natural selection, Newton's laws, or the standard model of elementary particle physics because they make no claim to being absolute truths, shoots itself in the foot.[30]

Just as religion finds itself challenging contemporary science when it identifies with discarded nature models, so it must expect to compete for hearts and minds with evolving social and political models when it clings to antiquated moral codes. Here the case is not as clear-cut as with most nature models because it is typically much harder to demonstrate the superiority of a new social, political, or moral model than it is of a new nature model. The evidence is often ambiguous, even contradictory, partly because shifting personal preferences play a much larger, and often hidden, role. As everyone who has argued politics is aware, the "facts" cited by partisans in support of their policy choices are often as debatable as the policies themselves.

Like nature models, political, social, and moral models originate in human experience, and, as experience accumulates, they evolve. Typically, the models we've inherited from the past were formulated over centuries, if not millennia. One reason that religious models generally lag behind the emerging social consensus is that the morals espoused by religion have usually proven useful over long periods of time and have become deeply entrenched. Hence, the first impulse is a conservative one, and often takes the form of shaming or coercing non-conformists into toeing the line.

The predilections of rebellious youth notwithstanding, tradition is not always wrong. What are now seen as traditional values earned their stripes in competition with alternative precepts that lost out. But, in basing morality on scripture, instead of evidence, people of faith reveal a lack of faith in the findings of their own sages and prophets. Instead, why not see these prophets as futurists and judge their prophecies against the evidence? The question then becomes: Are their predictions confirmed or contradicted by experience? The answer may not be immediately apparent, but looking for an answer in a context that respects evidence is a lot more productive than invoking ambiguous scripture on one side or the other.

In this view, the term "moral" does not gain its legitimacy by virtue of its status as "received wisdom," engraved in holy writ. Rather, the body of moral law is a prescriptive model of morality based on close observation, intuition, and extrapolation. Prophets like Moses, Buddha, Lao Tzu, Mo Tzu, Jesus, Mohammed, Sankara,[31] and others are seen as prescient moral philosophers with an uncanny knack for the long view.

As in science, virtually simultaneous, independent discovery of the same moral truths is not uncommon. Then and now, moral precepts can be understood as intuitive extrapolations based on empirical observations of cause and effect.

Take, for example, the commandment, "Thou shalt not kill." It's not hard to imagine that witnesses to tit-for-tat cycles of revenge killings concluded that "not killing" was the way to avoid deadly multi-generational feuds, and that someone—history credits Moses—packaged this discovery (along with other similar moral precepts) for his contemporaries and, unknowingly, for posterity.

From a modeling perspective, it's plausible that all ten commandments were assembled from the combined wisdom of people who, drawing on the oral and written history of past and current generations, and bearing close witness to their own psychological and emotional dynamics, realized that certain individual behaviors ran counter to personal stability and undermined group solidarity, thereby making the community vulnerable to exploitation and domination by more cohesive groups. They labeled these practices "immoral," anticipating that over time economic, psychological, social, and political forces would bring about either their elimination or relative decline of groups that countenanced them.

The Ten Commandments and other moral precepts are recorded in the world's holy books. Distilled and refined through the ages, they constitute the moral foundation of human societies. If somehow they were to disappear from consciousness and we had to start over (think of William Golding's novel *Lord of the Flies*), we would, by trial and error and with much bloodshed, gradually rediscover some of them from scratch and discard those that, in the meantime, circumstances had rendered obsolete.

Although some attribute moral principles to divine revelation, that's just one explanation and it's unverifiable. We may instead think of them as having been discovered in the same way that we discover everything else—through careful observation and verification. Having demonstrated their value in reducing suffering and/or in maintaining social stability, they were then elevated to special status, not unlike the process that results in the formulation and promulgation of successful science models, theories, rules, and laws.

A given rule of thumb can stand as shorthand for the whole body of observations and reasoning that undergirds it, in the same way that Newton's laws encapsulate classical dynamics. The moral principles of religion represent an accumulation of proverbial injunctions that function as reminders and ethical guides.

As with all models, so with models of morality: close follow-up scrutiny may bring exceptions to light. Exceptions have long been sanctioned to the commandment "Thou shalt not kill"—to wit, capital punishment and warfare. But Moses may yet have the last word. As we move into the twenty-first century, the global trend to abolish capital punishment is unmistakable. Likewise, the inefficacy of war as an instrument of foreign policy is becoming clearer, and, as it does, the frequency of wars is diminishing.[32]

Those who argue that religion should be counted out are overlooking the role that religious leaders played in overcoming segregation in America, repealing apartheid in South Africa, and ending the communist dictatorship in Poland and Central Europe. That religion has not always lived up to its own ideals does not mean it hasn't also made important contributions to social justice.

Religion is a repository of the time-tested wisdom of the ages, and a purveyor of precepts that have acquired the mantle of tradition. But as every reformer knows, tradition has its downside. Old moral codes can legitimize patterns of indignity; premonitions of a fairer world are then strangled in the crib. While the heavy hand of tradition saves us from our worst, too often it keeps us from our best.

Tradition and precedent, sometimes bolstered with assertions of infallibility, constitute a high hurdle that any new social or political model must clear. A case in point was the twentieth-century shift in the prevailing societal consensus on issues of race, gender, marriage, divorce, birth control, and sex. After decades of debate, new values gradually displaced older ones in the public mind. Where religious doctrine failed to adjust, the public gradually stopped paying attention. This has likely been a factor in the precipitous decline, since World War II, of church attendance in Europe. Over the long term, people increasingly look not to their church, synagogue, or mosque for their views on how to live and how to vote, but rather to culture and politics. This same trend is now becoming visible in the United States.[33]

When either science or religion allies itself with a partisan political doctrine—no matter if it's Left or Right—it weds itself to the biases of a particular time. That is what Soviet supporters of Lysenko did in the 1930s.[34] It's what phrenologists did in the nineteenth century.[35] It's what churchmen who supported Nazism did when they invoked religious beliefs in support of the state's nationalistic and anti-Semitic agenda.

Likewise, when religion attaches itself to social or political models—for example, racial segregation or sexual mores—it eventually loses relevance in those domains. To chain theology to the ship of state is to go down with the ship when it sinks. The nineteenth-century English biologist Thomas Henry Huxley, an early champion of Darwin's theory of evolution, pointed out that, in just this way, "Science commits suicide when it adopts a creed." Untold suffering is often the result of such partisan mistakes, and they are avoidable.

For example, when Alfred Kinsey's studies on sexuality revealed the full range of human sexual behavior, we had two choices. We could label some of the behaviors that came to light "perverted," and try to suppress them. Or, we could look upon them as falling within an enlarged domain of "normal" and modify our prescriptive models accordingly. The advent of reliable birth control only intensified the pressure to revise traditional sexual norms. The ensuing sexual revolution suggests that the public is moving toward a new consensus on sexuality.

What does this perspective suggest regarding the current debate about broadening the definition of marriage to include partners of the same sex?[36] In the end, the matter will be decided not by the victory of one or another interpretation of scripture, but by reference to emerging social values, very much as disagreements over slavery and, a century later, segregation, were decided. As it became clear that second-class citizenship was indefensible, attempts to justify these practices through religion were abandoned and instead other religious values were enlisted on behalf of emancipation and desegregation.

If barring same-sex marriage is viewed as an infringement on the civil rights of homosexuals, then the tide of history suggests that these barriers will fall. Despite frustratingly slow progress and numerous setbacks, it's hard to find examples of campaigns for equal minority rights—that is, movements to end second-class citizenship—that do not ultimately succeed. In the long run inclusiveness beats exclusiveness; dignity for all trumps indignity for some.[37] Religion could as well lay claim to this general insight (which it co-authored), and consistently champion the indignified, as give its blessing to one or another kind of second-class citizenship. The idea of evolving truth is a keystone of universal dignity. Humility is not simply a trait to be admired; it's required by the fact that there are viable, sometimes better, alternatives to our traditional ways of doing things.

The movement toward more inclusive, participatory models of governance shows no signs of abating in the twenty-first century. Protests for dignity and democracy have erupted in the Middle East, Russia, Burma, China, and, in the form of the Occupy Movement, across North America.

Let's take a moment to consider what it would take for religion and science to end their stand-off and support each other in the pursuit of universal dignity.

A New Deal for Science and Religion

Moral laws can be seen as intuitions, based on observation, that are then elevated to absolute truths. It's the elevation to absolutes that leads to trouble, not the intuitive guesswork that's common to discoveries of all kinds. So, one way to resolve the perennial war between science and religion is for religion to accept science's methodology and defend religious precepts much as scientists defend theirs. In such a framework, both science and religion would reserve the right to speculate and, before expecting others to accept their findings, they'd assume responsibility for demonstrating the validity of their ideas and theories by marshaling evidence for their support.

Such an understanding does not preclude specialization. Religion is free to imagine new worlds and to suggest things it cannot prove. Guessing the answer is a respected way of doing science and so scientists don't have a leg to stand on when they dismiss religion as guesswork.

> First you guess. Don't laugh, this is the most important step. Then you compute the consequences. Compare the consequences to experience. If it disagrees with experience, the guess is wrong. In that simple statement is the key to science. It doesn't matter how beautiful your guess is or how smart you are or what your name is. If it disagrees with experience, it's wrong. That's all there is to it.
>
> – Richard Feynman

Science tests such guesses and intuitions against the evidence. Religion can do no less.

Under the terms of this deal, religion would be more humble about its teachings, acknowledging that they are sometimes wrong. When a hypothesis is disproven, religion would gracefully accept the result and propose something else. When science confirms one of religion's guesses, it gives credit where credit is due for having "divined" the answer before it could be established beyond doubt (that is, verified to the satisfaction of investigators who were initially neutral or skeptical).

In time, science and religion would come to see each other as complementary aspects of a single truth-seeking strategy. Religion specializes in identifying cutting-edge, revelatory, intuitive insights into human psychological and social dynamics (seemingly out of thin air, but actually, intuitively, after a lot of close observation). For its part, science specializes in testing these insights against the evidence, and either disproving or confirming them. Both vocations are at liberty to encroach on the other's traditional turf.

Under this arrangement, science and religion would likely retain something of their traditional flavors, but gradually each would incorporate into its practice the others' perspective. With the roles of science and religion clarified, their relationship would be characterized by mutual respect and collaboration. On matters for which there is insufficient evidence, people would be free to disagree. The difference, though, is that they would cease to berate and demean each other. Such a change in attitude and atmospherics was an important step in ending the Cold War between the U.S. and the U.S.S.R., and it will likely also be required to end hostilities between science and religion.

By interpreting religious principles not as holy, inerrant writ, but as fallible truths that are discovered in the same way as other truths, religion can defend itself against accusations that it is just another self-serving institution, and, by assuming a leadership role in the transition to a post-predatory world, it can help realize the prophetic vision of peace on Earth, goodwill toward men.

For centuries, religion has met peoples' emotional needs with its art and music, its theater and counsel. This will no doubt continue. But, as dignity's discoverer and its defender of last resort, a new revivifying role for religion can be envisioned. In it, religion would:

- Provide a forum for debating and disseminating proposed models of morality

- Research and develop models that extend dignity to people subjected to indignity

- Facilitate society-wide and world-wide conversations aimed at defining exactly what is meant by "equal dignity for all" (until a broad consensus is achieved)

- Assume the role of coach to organizations as they bring their practices in line with dignity-affirming values

- Support the dignity movement as it did the civil rights movement

- Teach the latest findings on the workings of the mind and the dynamics of self-transformation

- Offer enlightenment and creativity training (analogous to literacy training)

- Support scientific and spiritual seekers by reminding them of the mythic nature of the quest for truth

- Imagine better futures—such as the brotherhood of man—and ennoble our quests to realize those dreams

With the prospect of a beautiful friendship between science and religion, there is indeed reason to hope.

Chapter 7: The Peace Dividend

Somebodies and Nobodies

Bullying has always bothered me. Not just being bullied, though that too of course. I mean the *phenomenon* of bullying, in all its forms. I think bullying troubles everyone, even the bullies themselves. No one wants to be pushed around, to be forced to act against one's own interests. And, if it's happening to anyone, deep down we know it can happen to us.

Growing up, I saw bullying all around me. War was an extreme example of it. Slavery was, too. But, I didn't need to look that far afield to find bullies. My schools were full of put downs, physical and verbal. Some of my classmates were regularly humiliated with epithets like "retard" and "fatso." In college and graduate school, one-upmanship was the name of the game. Women were actively discouraged from studying mathematics and physics. Some educators even went so far as to claim that females lacked the "math gene."

And, of course, in mid-century America everyone knew that blacks could be denigrated at will. When our all-white high school athletic teams lost to a school with black players, the N-word was employed to remind African Americans of their inferior social rank.

By the 1960s, the growing strength of the civil rights movement was forcing Americans to question race-based discrimination. Within a few years, other liberation movements took aim at the indignities that were routinely visited upon women, the elderly, homosexuals, and people with disabilities.

As a college president in the early 1970s, it was my responsibility to handle the grievances of various identity groups, I sensed that all of them had something in common—namely, those targeted for discrimination were taken for "nobodies" by their victimizers, who in turn saw themselves as "somebodies." But, rank was relative. You could be a somebody in one context and a nobody in another. Somebodies could pull rank on nobodies, of course, but equally significant was that nobodies could lord it over people of still lower rank.It was the *power* attached to rank that made degradation, discrimination, and abuse possible. If, by virtue of your place in a social or organizational hierarchy, you outranked someone, then the power of your rank shielded you from retaliation.

Identity politics had been effective at curtailing indignities that targeted solidarity groups defined by a common trait, but it was impotent when it came to disallowing indignities *within* these groups. My ah-ha was that all of the familiar isms were special cases of rank-based abuse and that, even taken together, they represented just the tip of the indignity iceberg.

But not to despair. In combatting racism, sexism, ageism, etc. techniques had been battle-tested that could now be leveled against the basic source of a wide variety of indignities—the abuse of power vested in rank.

Given the achievements of the identity-based liberation movements, is it unrealistic to imagine a day when everyone's equal dignity will be as self-evident as everyone's right to "life, liberty, and the pursuit of happiness?"[38] If one racial group can learn to treat members of another race with dignity, why can't it learn to treat people of the same race with dignity? The same applies to gender and the other traits that have served as pretexts for abuse and discrimination. If we can learn not to put people down who carry certain defining traits, why can't we learn not to put anyone down?

That we've found ways to curb the indignities suffered by minorities, women, gays, the elderly, and people with disabilities suggests that making dignity the norm universally may not be out of reach. We could teach kids that dignity is their right and that it's also everyone else's. *We could teach everyone to defend the dignity of others as they would have others defend theirs.*

When I heard this proposition sounding in my head, I recognized it as an echo of the rule we'd mouthed in Sunday School. But in those days, although we were exhorted to obey the golden rule, no one seemed bound by it, not even the teachers and preachers who urged it upon others.

Since then, liberation movements—as personified by Mahatma Gandhi and Nelson Mandela, Martin Luther King Jr., Betty Friedan, and others—have done more to put violations of the golden rule on the defensive than centuries of preaching. What if the techniques of identity politics were applied not just in defense of the dignity of minorities, women, and gays, but to identify and overcome all forms of indignity?

The rest of this chapter sketches a model of morality that, by pinning a name on the rank-based abuse that causes indignity, addresses one of my take-away questions from Sunday School: How could we make the golden rule not only self-evident, but self-enforcing?

A Model of Morality

As mentioned in the discussion of modeling, the natural sciences search for grand unifying theories, also referred to as "theories of everything," or TOEs. Everything? you may wonder. Really, everything?

Well, no, not quite everything. Not why some people like blueberries and hate broccoli, and for others, it's vice versa. Not who will win the World Series next year. Not the answer to the question Einstein said would be his first if he returned in 500 years: "Is the universe friendly?" Chalk up that word—everything—to poetic license. What scientists mean by a TOE is a theory that explains everything that current narrower theories do, but goes on to explain something more. In other words, a TOE is a broader, more inclusive, theory, a theory of greater generality.

Whether it's a theory of nature or human behavior, TOEs are important because they give us insight into the unruly margins where models of lesser scope break down. For example, by examining the intersection of the fields of electricity and magnetism, Maxwell discovered a broader theory that revealed that light was an electromagnetic wave and accurately predicted its speed. Radio was one of the early applications of Maxwell's theory. When Newton's laws of classical mechanics and Maxwell's electromagnetic theory were applied to the atom, they gave false results, but in the hands of Niels Bohr a new theory emerged—the quantum theory of the atom—that opened up the hitherto unexplored world of atomic physics. Similarly, when Paul Dirac married quantum mechanics and relativity, his more general theory predicted a new family of elementary particles, known as antiparticles. In the natural sciences, nothing hollers "Nobel Prize" louder than a TOE.

A more modest acronym for the Moral TOE I'll explore in this chapter would be MOM—Model Of Morality. (Think of "MOM" as acknowledging the mothers of the world who model morality for their children. Although, I shall speak of TOEs and MOMs, it's not without a dollop of irony, as the acronyms are meant to suggest.)

Models are sitting ducks—meant to be faulted and disproven. Like all models, the MOM I shall sketch immediately becomes a legitimate target: What does it not account for? What does it get wrong? After all, its certain destiny is to be replaced by a better MOM. But if this MOM serves to provoke others to come up with something better, then it will be worth whatever mockery it provokes.

In the spirit of full disclosure and minimal obfuscation, I'm going to reverse the usual practice and give away my MOM's punch line up front. Like the truths of science, it is disconcertingly simple, yet has a host of non-obvious, far-reaching implications.

When science and religion stop fighting and pool their findings, the headline and bottom line of the MOM that leaps out at us will be:

Dignity for All, Always

What People Want—Dignity

There's a place for us,
A time and place for us.
Hold my hand and we're half way there.
Hold my hand and I'll take you there
Somehow, Someday, Somewhere!

– Stephen Sondheim, *West Side Story*

What people really want in relationships is dignity, not domination. While it's not hard to understand why people who have suffered oppression might fantasize taking a turn at domination, to actually do so is to over-reach. Domination is not a reciprocal, symmetrical relationship. It's one of superior and inferior, and simply reversing roles of sovereign and subject perpetuates indignity rather than ends it. Reversing the directionality of domination is not a long-term equilibrium solution to inequity, indignity, and injustice. Like other revenge-driven "peace" arrangements, it invariably unravels and the struggle for domination resumes.

Dignity is in a class by itself when it comes to establishing good relationships with our fellow humans. Why? What is meant by dignity?

Each of us has an innate sense that we have the same inherent worth as anyone else, regardless of our individual traits or worldly status. Though religious practice may deny equality of dignity—there are, for example, plenty of sexist precepts in the world's holy books much as there are many abandoned theories in the world's scientific books—these same holy books also teach that dignity is a birthright that cannot be annulled by any person, circumstance, institution, or government. That God does not play favorites is an article of faith common to most religions, and the source of the egalitarian ideals to which governments of every stripe feel required to pay lip service.

Indignity—An Existential Threat

Dignity is not negotiable.

– Vartan Gregorian

Like other animals vulnerable to being preyed upon, we're supersensitive to threats to our well-being. Among our ancestors, those who missed signs of predatory intent became someone's lunch.[39]

For this same reason, we're alert to subtle attempts to determine our relative strength, from "innocent" opening lines such as "And you are?" or "Who are you with?" to more probing queries regarding our ancestry or education. All it takes is a faint whiff of presumed superiority or condescension and we're on guard.

Indeed, we're often unaware of our dignity until it *is* slighted. We know at once when we're treated with disrespect, and for good reason. An intimation or overt gesture of disregard may be a test to gauge our resistance to subservience, or to put us in our place. An insult is often a precursor to ostracism, to casting us as a nobody. Whole groups may be marginalized, as well as individuals. *Indignity is an existential threat.* No wonder we're so quick to register it!

While those atop the social pyramid prize liberty above all, most people put dignity first. History is full of examples of humiliated peoples who willingly surrender their freedom to a demagogue promising to restore their pride. One has only to think of Weimar Germany in the aftermath of the punitive Versailles treaty that concluded World War I.

The need for dignity is more than a desire for respect. Dignity grounds us, nurtures us, protects us. It's the social counterpart of interpersonal love. To affirm people's dignity confirms their status as valued members of a group. Dignity and self-respect go hand in hand: dignity nourishes our self-respect, and self-respect inclines others to affirm our dignity.

By protecting the dignity of others as if it were our own, we not only give others their due, we simultaneously protect ourselves by not giving offense in the first place.

Every child knows that indignities flow downstream—from "somebodies" of higher rank (indicating greater power) to "nobodies" of lower rank (and relatively less power). No sooner do we understand this, than we imagine a solution: eliminate ranks that signify degrees of power.

But power differences are a fact of life. To bemoan them is like complaining that the sun is brighter than the moon. When rank differences reflect power differences, they cannot be wished away.

Fortunately, this stark reality does not doom the prospects of achieving equal dignity for all. In and of itself, rank is *not* a source of indignity. Unless rank is inherently illegitimate—as, for example, specious social rankings that foist second-class citizenship on particular identity groups—then the problem is not with rank per se but rather with its abuse. The distinction between rank and its abuse goes to the heart of many vexing and intractable political issues, domestic and international. In most cases, indignity has its origins in *abuse* of the power signified by rank.

Confusing rank with its abuse occurs because rank is so commonly misused that young and old alike jump to the conclusion that the only remedy is to abolish ranking. Conflating rank and rank-based abuse is logically unnecessary and it's a mistake with grave consequences. The socialists of nineteenth-century Europe and communists of the twentieth century often suffered from, or cynically exploited, this misconception.

When egalitarian ideologies did prevail, the self-appointed leaders typically imposed even harsher tyrannies than the ones they replaced. This was the Soviet Union's Achilles' heel.

When it is legitimately earned and properly used, rank can be a useful organizational tool for achieving group goals. We rightfully admire and love authorities—parents, teachers, bosses, even political leaders—who use the power of their rank in exemplary ways.

Accepting such leadership entails no loss of self-respect or opportunity by those in subordinate roles. It is when people use the power of their position to aggrandize themselves or disadvantage those they outrank that seeds of indignity are sown.

Dignity is a universal desire, not something that liberals favor and conservatives oppose or vice versa. Every religion supports dignity for all in principle, if not always in practice.

Equal dignity is grounded in the fact of our dependence upon specialization and cooperation for survival, or, more fundamentally, in the co-creation of our very identities. This suggests that both the Left and the Right have equal stakes in, and responsibility for, universalizing dignity

Rankism—The Source of Indignity

To have a name is to be.

– Benoit Mandelbrot[40]

A key insight of identity politics is the importance of *naming the malady you want to cure.*[41] When women pinned the label "sexism" on the attitudes and practices that had long kept them down, those practices became targetable. In the last half-century, identity politics has given a name to a half-dozen trait-based abuses and delegitimized every one of them. Eradicating a malady takes longer, of course, but it begins with the delegitimization that naming makes possible.

Absent a name for rank-based abuses, targets were in a position similar to that of women before the term "sexism" was coined. Writing in 1963, Betty Friedan characterized the plight of women as "the problem that has no name."[42] By 1968, the problem had acquired one—"sexism."[43] That simple word intensified consciousness-raising and public debate and provided a rallying cry for a movement to oppose power-abuse linked to gender.

When abuse and discrimination are race-based, we call it racism; when they're age-based, we call it ageism. By analogy, abuse of the power attached to rank is *rankism*.

Once there's a name for it, you see it everywhere. And once it's visible, its legitimacy can be questioned.

The relationship between rankism and the various isms targeted by identity politics can be compared to that between cancer and its subspecies. For centuries the group of diseases that are now seen as subspecies of cancer were regarded as distinct illnesses. No one realized that lung, breast, and other organ-specific malignancies all had their origins in cellular malfunction.

In this metaphor, racism, sexism, homophobia, and other varieties of prejudice are analogous to organ-specific cancers, and rankism is the generic malady analogous to cancer itself. Now that it has a name, it's easier for victims of rankism to stand up for their dignity. Once victims are on their feet, they rarely stand down until their demands are met.

Religion divined the golden rule thousands of years ago, but has not been able to bring about its widespread observance. In every society and every religion, leaders have downplayed, if not ignored, its implication of dignity for all and instead lent moral support to the degradation of racial and ethnic minorities, colonial subjects, women and girls, and homosexuals.

The twentieth century witnessed the successful application of the strategies and tactics of identity politics. Those same organizational techniques, applied to overcoming rankism, can render it as insupportable as the isms that identity politics has now put on the defensive.

Imagine what it would mean if the golden rule were to become the new default state for interpersonal and social relations.

The Many Faces of Rankism

Rankism is a collective name for the various ways power can be abused in the context of a rank difference. It's a name broad enough to cover a wide range of rank-based indignities and abuses. Whereas, rank is meant to serve, rankism is self-serving, a perversion of service.Examples of rankism (some may overlap):

- Illegitimate use of rank (e.g., a boss extorting money or sex from an employee)

- The creation or use of social hierarchies that condone degradation and exploitation (e.g., the social construct of white superiority and supremacy; the caste system; patriarchy)

- Damaging or degrading assertions of rank (e.g., name-calling, mugging, sexual harassment, priest abuse, *droit du seigneur,* and Eve teasing)

- Actions or social arrangements that violate the principle of equal dignity (e.g., racial segregation, lack of the franchise)

- Putting others down; disempowering them (name-calling; obfuscation by elites)

- Using the power inherent in rank to strengthen the hold on a senior position or otherwise advantage incumbents (e.g., office-holders exploiting the advantages of incumbency to insure retention of rank; life-time appointments that leave tenured teachers, professors, judges, and clerics virtually unaccountable)

- Self-service as contrasted to serving the avowed purpose of the organization (e.g., executives awarding themselves bonuses not on the basis of performance, but simply by virtue of their power to get away with doing so)

- Using the power of rank not to empower others, but to promote, enrich, or empower oneself (e.g., predatory lending)

I hope you'll add to this list.

In many cases, ranking serves no purpose other than to create and maintain the privileges of the high-ranking. Often rank merely signifies seniority, not degrees of expertise. Although ranking is not inherently rankist, it's often used as a cover for institutionalizing discrimination, for example, in aristocracies, caste systems, and schools. Hierarchies are famously prone to ensuring the privileges of rank-holders, to the detriment of those served.

Varieties of Rankism

Racism	Torture	Sexual Harassment
Sexism	Trafficking	Anti-Semitism
Ageism	Corruption	Classism
Homophobia	Influence Peddling	Childism[44]
Ableism	Graft	Exceptionalism
Bullying	Nepotism	Speciesism[45]
Slavery	Tenure	Paternalism
Elder Abuse	Rape	Condescension
Prisoner Abuse	Sexual Abuse	One-upmanship

The Golden Rule in the Model of Morality

The centerpiece of this model of morality is "Dignity for All, Always." Look around and you'll see that the world is manifestly in violation of this precept: predation and the consequences thereof—indignity—are everywhere.

But, despair not. The fact that we have successfully disallowed subspecies of predatory practice suggests that we might be able to give up predation itself. Though they've not been eliminated, many of the most egregious forms of predation have been made illegal. Delegitimizing residual predation, by disallowing rankism, would usher in a *dignitarian* era in human history, an era in which we're obliged to protect the dignity of others as we would have them respect and protect ours. Dignitarian politics gives the golden rule teeth—by naming indignities and so making them targetable. Together, science, religion, and politics could, plausibly, retire the predatory survival strategy, which has been characteristic of *Homo sapiens* until now, in favor of a dignitarian strategy that would characterize our species going forward.

The manifest righteousness of the golden rule has long posed a psychological barrier to inflicting indignity on our fellow humans. The lengths to which we've gone to justify predatory behaviors reveals our unease with contravening it. The excuses we invent to create loopholes to the golden rule are graduated in proportion to the degree of the indignity we inflict. For example, we *demonize* our enemies to justify killing them; we *dehumanize* captives to justify enslaving them; we *degrade* victims of discrimination to rationalize exploiting them; we *dismiss* people as nobodies to justify discounting their views.

So long as our individual survival depended on out-competing rivals for scarce necessities, we availed ourselves of excuses like these to suspend our intuition of the brotherhood of man and free ourselves to prey on our human kin. But, the fact that we don't flout the golden rule without feeling the need to justify ourselves suggests that if these excuses were disallowed, the rule might become largely self-enforcing. That's exactly what having a collective name—rankism—for the various causes of indignity can help us do. As mentioned, having the word *sexism* in the lexicon helped to disallow excuses for discrimination against women. In a similar way, might not the word rankism enable us to spotlight residual rank-based abuses of power and put perpetrators on the defensive?

The self-evident nature of the golden rule and the success of Einstein's relativity theory both have their origins in underlying symmetries. As the poet says, "Beauty is truth, truth beauty."[46] Mathematicians have discovered that the connection between truth and beauty lies in symmetry.[47]

The symmetry undergirding the golden rule is the assumption of equal dignity for all. The symmetry underlying the theory of relativity is the assumption of equal validity of reference frames (of other observers). A deeper understanding of our place in the cosmos will likely shed further light on the role of symmetry in shaping both physical and moral law.

When, in 1915, Einstein succeeded in generalizing his theory of special relativity to general relativity, he was rewarded by a theory of gravitation that improved upon Newton's classical laws of motion. So, too, when identity politics is generalized to apply to all victims of degradation (not just those distinguished by a trait like color, gender, age, etc.) then we're rewarded with a universal theory of morality. The analogue of Einstein's assumptions—that one reference frame is as good as another and the speed of light is the same in all of them—is the assumption of equal dignity for all people regardless of role or rank. Since indignity is caused by rankism, it follows from the assumption of equal dignity that the model of morality delegitimizes rankism.

So long as we see our "self" as a target that must defend itself against indignities, we're likely to respond in kind. "An eye for an eye, a tooth for a tooth" is, among other things, the fundamental law of reciprocal indignity. But, if we see our "self" as nimble and porous, we can sidestep arrows with our name on them and respond to indignities in a way that does not attack the dignity of those who trespass against us. Breaking the cycle of indignity and violence is a dignitarian application of "turn the other cheek." As reciprocal dignity becomes the norm, the roles we play in co-creating and maintaining each others' identities become clear, and "love thy neighbor as thyself" begins to look like an obtainable ideal.

While the twentieth century saw progress in overcoming certain sub-species of rankism, many varieties of it persist unchecked. Reasons for pessimism and despair are not hard to come by. Since World War II there have been scores of wars, millions of casualties, tens of millions of refugees; fighting continues today in many parts of the world. Since the Holocaust, and despite the world's determination that it not happen again, genocides have occurred in Cambodia, Rwanda, Bosnia, Darfur, and elsewhere. Poverty enshrouds one-third of the world's seven billion people and experts warn that population pressure and/or climate change will pit us against each other in a struggle for scarce resources.

Many insist that man's predatory practices are undiminished and ineradicable. But an opposing trend is becoming visible. While admitting that "the arc of the moral universe is long," Martin Luther King, Jr. believed that "it bends toward justice."

In the final chapter, we take up the question of whether or not King's dream might be realized. Did he, do we, have reason to hope for "peace on Earth, goodwill toward men," or is the brotherhood of man a pipe dream?

Chapter 8: The Brotherhood of Man

The Moral Arc of History and the Golden Rule

The arc of the moral universe is long but it bends toward justice.

  – Martin Luther King, Jr.

One reading of the human story emphasizes war, domination, pillage, rape, slavery, colonization, and exploitation. Wealth and leisure for the few and a subsistence living for the many. To the extent that we can put people down and keep them there, we take what's theirs and force them to do our bidding. To the extent that we can't credibly do so, it's our ineluctable fate to be victims.

Another telling of history highlights overthrowing tyrants, expelling colonizers, and, by marshaling the strength of numbers, progressively emancipating ourselves from slavery, poverty, and other forms of degradation.

The key to deciding which of these perspectives is predictive of the human future lies in a paradoxical property of power. Once it's understood that a group's competitive success vis à vis *other* groups depends on limiting abuses of power *within* the group, King's optimism regarding the curvature of the moral arc of history is vindicated.

Here's the gist of the argument: If a ruler is regarded as unjust or self-aggrandizing by his subjects, morale will deteriorate to the point that group solidarity is weakened and the will to defend the group is impaired. Unjust leaders neither deserve nor elicit loyalty and, when push comes to shove, their people turn on them.

This means that governance that promotes loyalty and solidarity has survival value. Even societies that adopt a *predatory* stance looking outwards, are short-sighted if they disregard *dignitarian* values looking inwards. Over the course of history, not to complement outward-directed predatory capability with a modicum of dignity for those within the group has been to lose out to groups whose stronger social bond enabled them to marshal and project superior force.

For this reason, upholding dignity is more than an admonition to be "nice." A policy of relatively equal dignity enhances the power of groups that practice it. None do so consistently, of course, but some do so more than others, and this gives them a competitive advantage stemming from social cohesiveness. This suggests that, on a millennial time scale, the golden rule is self-enforcing. We were too quick to judge it toothless. Rather, it simply took a few thousand years to cut teeth.

As we realize that over the long haul dignitarian societies have a competitive advantage, and as less dignitarian groups are absorbed by more dignitarian ones, we operationalize the golden rule and extend its writ.

It's important to recognize that within groups it's not just "top dogs" who abuse power. Power abuse is a tempting strategy at any rank because everybody is a somebody to someone and a nobody to someone else. Accordingly, a predatory posture can be assumed toward underlings no matter where one stands in a hierarchy.[48]

Because societies predicated on equal dignity are more productive and creative, and are more strongly committed to their common cause—be it aggressive or defensive—they are, on average, fitter. This does not mean that dignitarian groups win every contest with more predatory groups. Factors other than social cohesion also figure in the outcome. But it does mean that, with starts and fits, organizations and states that tolerate power abuses effectively de-select themselves.[49] Over a long enough time period, the circle of dignity expands.

The paradox of power is that, statistically, dignitarian societies gradually absorb less dignitarian ones until finally there is no longer a significant likelihood of inter-group predation. Disgruntled outliers may resort to violence or disruption, but they will not be successful unless they are serving as proxies for a larger group that shares their grievances and their indignation.

A selection process governed by the same dynamic unfolds among organizations. For example, more dignitarian companies will, on average, serve their customers and employees better, and will outperform less dignitarian ones. In a phrase, dignity works, indignity doesn't.

While the evolutionary trend prophesied by Martin Luther King Jr. may at first sound like wishful thinking, it is revealed as a logical consequence of the free play of power within and among competing groups. The paradox of power—that in the long run, right makes might, not vice versa—provides causal underpinning for optimism regarding the curvature of the moral universe. Despite the relentless drumbeat of bad news, the twenty-first century could witness the gradual phasing out of our age-old predatory strategy and the adoption of a dignitarian one. Even if there are major setbacks—and we must expect reversals and prepare for them—there is reason to believe that the state toward which humankind is tending is one of universal dignity.

Is Competition Compatible with Dignity for All?

There's a conceptual barrier to putting our predatory past behind us, and not to address it would be remiss in a book claiming there is reason to hope.

Disallowing predation sounds utopian to many because, as a society, we haven't quite figured out how to forego habitual predatory behavior without inhibiting competition. Although it's natural to see competition as the culprit (because it is so very often unfair, and because many competitors interpret winning a particular competition as an excuse for demeaning and exploiting those who lose), no society that has curtailed competition has long endured. As libertarian ideology confuses predation with competition and may find itself an apologist for the former, so egalitarian ideology confuses competition with predation and may advocate killing the goose—competition— that lays the golden egg. To this dilemma—how to allow competition while disallowing predation—dignitarian ethics provides a possible solution.

Competition is an integral part of our past and fair competition is indispensable to a prosperous, robust future. To delegitimize gradations of power is not only impossible, it's a recipe for dysfunction. Fair competition is in fact one of the best safeguards against rankism ever devised.

From the natural selection that drives the differentiation of species to the marketplace that refines products and ideas, competition determines fitness and protects us from abuses of power by economic and political monopolies. To abolish competition is to invite stagnation, and eventually to fall behind societies that hone their competitive edge.

The difference between predation and competition is that predation knows no rules. In contrast, competition can be made fair. In athletic contests, we do this by having referees to enforce the rules evenhandedly. Making sure that competition is fair—by disallowing rankism in all its guises—is a proper function of government.

At every point in our social evolution, power rules. Power is neither good nor bad, it just is, and trying to eliminate power differences is barking up the wrong tree. *Abuses* of power, however, are something else. They will persist only so long as the individuals or institutions perpetrating them wield greater power. This would be grounds for cynicism were it not that when power is abused there eventually surfaces a less abusive and therefore ultimately more powerful alternative. Groups that harbor indignity burden themselves with the corrosive effects of suppressed indignation. The long-term trend of this evolutionary process is the discovery of ever more effective forms of cooperation, successively out-producing, out-performing, and finally replacing more rankist organizations, institutions, societies, and states.

Dr. King's intuition regarding the curvature of the moral universe is correct: it bends toward justice.

The Dawning of a Dignitarian Era
As prophets in every religion have tried to tell us, humankind is one big extended family. The simultaneous advent of globalization and the emergence of dignitarian values is no coincidence. Greater exposure to "foreigners" is making their demonization untenable, and the predatory strategy is becoming obsolete.

An important factor in its demise is that it simply isn't working as well as it used to. Victims of rankism have gained access to powerful modern weapons and can exact a high price for humiliations inflicted on them. Increasingly, they're in a position to make the cost of predation exceed the value of the spoils. Weapons of mass destruction seize the imagination, but even if they're never used, non-violent "weapons" of mass *disruption*, employed by aggrieved groups, can paralyze modern, highly interdependent societies. This represents a fundamental shift in the balance of power in favor of the disregarded, disenfranchised, and dispossessed.

Given that predation has been a fixture throughout human history, it's not surprising that when one form of predation has ceased to work, we've devised alternative, subtler forms to accomplish the same thing. Although slavery itself is no longer defended, poverty functions in much the same way— by institutionalizing the domination and exploitation of the poorer by the richer. As Reverend Jim Wallis says, "Poverty is the new slavery."[50]

We shouldn't be surprised if, using techniques of mass disruption and tactics of non-violent civil disobedience, the poor make their continued exploitation untenable. The Occupy Movement, like the Arab Spring, appears to be a harbinger of a worldwide awakening to the inviolability of dignity.

Although moral precepts point the way, politics will play an indispensable role in setting aside predatory habits in favor of dignitarian ones. The next section shows the role that traditional Left and Right will have in crafting legislation to make "Dignity for All" the world's new default position and so, finally, realize religion's ancient dream of the brotherhood of man.

The Politics of Dignity

The tendency of societies to divide into two opposing partisan camps—conservative and liberal, republican and democrat, Right and Left—is universal and, in democracies, usually results in the parties taking turns in power.[51]

Simply declaring one party or the other wrongheaded fails to understand the complementary roles played by each. Both political orientations must serve a purpose or one would long-since have withered away. What purposes do the Left and the Right serve?

Partisanship has roots in the legitimate issue of how much authority to vest in rank. The Right has traditionally been the party that defends the authority and prerogatives of the propertied classes; the Left the party that would place limits on the power and privileges of those exercising authority. Accordingly, the Right tends to oppose, and the Left support, legislation that would make it easier for "nobodies" to hold accountable those entrusted with power. In the hurly-burly of history, the labels of Right and Left occasionally reverse. When the Bolsheviks, the party of the Left, seized power during the Russian Revolution of 1917, they abolished all constraints on governmental power.

Since both political persuasions have a valid role in good management, it's not surprising that democratic electorates tilt first one way and then the other, like a navigator who makes a continual series of course corrections to avoid beaching the ship (of state) on the shoals (of extremism).

Which party fulfills the progressive or conservative role is secondary compared to the overarching need to maintain social and political stability while avoiding autocracy and stasis. A society that can't trust anyone with power loses its ability to carry out complex tasks in a timely fashion. Systems of governance that cannot "stop people talking," in Clement Atlee's phrase, are vulnerable to what the women's movement called the "tyranny of structurelessness," which often takes the form of interminable, inconclusive meetings. On the other hand, societies that don't limit the power of their rulers (such as the USSR and Nazi Germany) find individual initiative stifled and liberty extinguished in a brutal tyranny of conformity.

Aversion to abuses of power can blind liberals to rank's legitimate functions. Likewise, attachment to the status quo can turn conservatives into apologists for rank's misuse.[52] To paraphrase an unknown pundit, we have lunatic fringes so we know how far *not* to go.[53]

The dignitarian strategy is to put rank and the power it signifies in the spotlight, and so make abuses of power, and the indignities resulting therefrom, indefensible. It sees a world of equal dignity as a steppingstone to the more just, fair, and decent societies[54] long foreseen by dreamers who prophesied the brotherhood of man.

The French revolutionary slogan "Liberty, Equality, Fraternity" overlooks the sine qua non of social harmony—*Dignity*. A persistent lack of dignity breeds indignation. Blowback may be suppressed for a time, but indignities, once lodged in the breast, fester until the aggrieved person, group, or nation sees a chance to get even.

No political theory predicated on either liberal or conservative values, qualifies as a TOE. By showing where each party's attitude toward authority is relevant, a dignitarian analysis locates libertarian, egalitarian, and fraternitarian values within a new larger synthesis—the politics of dignity. Dignitarian politics, which finds its ultimate rationale in the co-creation and mutual maintenance of both our persons and our personas, subordinates the agendas of both the Left and the Right to the task of establishing dignity for all, here and now.

The adoption of dignity as an inviolate political right marks a change fundamental enough to mark an era. Opportunistic predation—the survival strategy that we've long taken for human nature—has reached its "sell-by" date. Even wars by superpowers against much weaker states are proving unwinnable. When the long-term costs are taken into account, domination is not profitable.

Rankism is the residue of predation. Humanity's next step is to build dignitarian societies by overcoming rankism. Knowing that the moral arc of history bends toward justice gives reason to hope that the religious intuition of universal dignity is an achievable social condition.

If science and religion cooperate to uphold and extend dignity, and Left and Right remove the inequities that thwart fair competition, we can build a global society that's as close to heaven as we have need for, and realize the brotherhood of man not merely in our dreams, but here on Earth, not in the indefinite future, but before this century is out.

AFTERWORD

We are as gods and have to get good at it.

– Stewart Brand[55]

The shift from opportunistic predation to inviolate universal dignity is an epochal one, and arguably, it's one we now find ourselves making. However, it's only prudent to ask "What could go wrong? What could postpone the dawning of a dignitarian world? Are we overlooking new threats to human dignity?"

Challenges

[Someday human intelligence] might be viewed as a historically interesting, albeit peripheral, special case of machine intelligence.

– Pierre Baldi[56]

Futurists are warning that at some point during this century we'll be confronted with an unprecedented threat to what it means to be human—the advent of sophisticated thinking machines.[57] It's one thing to use calculators that outperform us; it would be quite another to face machines manifesting supra-human intelligence. Picture a cute little gadget perched on your desk who, by any measure, outperforms the cleverest, most creative person you know. We'll probably program such devices not to condescend to us, but the knowledge that they can beat us at our own game would take some getting used to.

A preview of how we're apt to react to such a development is provided by looking at how we have responded to prior demotions in status. Copernicus's removing the Earth, and us along with it, from center stage caused an uproar that lasted for centuries. Darwin's depiction of us as descendants of apes was initially scorned and is still rejected by some. If, as now seems likely, life is discovered in various stages of development on other planets, the effect will be to further undermine human claims to a special role.

In the face of these previous humblings, humans found what appeared to be an incontestable basis for pride in their superior intelligence. How will it affect our identity if we're pushed off *that* pedestal? We've rarely handled such blows with grace.

Faced with creations of our own making that outdo us, and notwithstanding a few valedictory tantrums, we'll probably end up by humbly accepting the help of thinking machines much as aging parents reluctantly accept advice from their grown offspring.

Over time, what is most distinctive and precious about human beings could be preserved and incorporated into the machines that, with help from our clever progeny, may someday supersede us. Dignity will be challenged, yes, but expunged? Not by smart machines, if we have the grace to make them our allies.

If the current trend toward dignity is reversed, it will likely be due to scarcity thrust upon us by our own actions. Obviously, the advent of a dignitarian world could be set back for decades, possibly centuries, by global economic collapse, war, pandemic, catastrophic climate change, and a host of other eventualities that could reinstate predatory competition for scarce resources. Though such calamities might slow the universalization of dignity, they are unlikely to permanently reverse a trend that can now be read between the lines on every page of the human story.

In the context of future challenges, it's illuminating to consider the proverb "The poor shall always be with you." Does "poor" refer literally to wealth, that is, does this proverb deny the possibility of an equitable world?

We could take the saying to mean that even if everyone has enough, there will always be variations in wealth, that is, there will remain some who are *relatively* poor. Or, we could take it to mean that although there may be no significant variations in financial security, there would still exist people who are poor in spirit, who lack recognition, or are lonely or otherwise unfulfilled. I find this maxim to be one of religion's more provocative hypotheses. I hope it's wrong, in both senses, but it's too early to tell. We do seem to be getting a handle on malnutrition, and it's not impossible that we'll eliminate it entirely and go on to address the damage done by malrecognition. Success against both "maladies" would offer hope that the poor will not always be with us.

Likewise, with the admonition "Love thy enemies."[58] It sounds like a bridge too far in today's world, but in a dignitarian world, where synthesis is the name of the game, love will be much closer to hand. Once again, religion is likely prophetic: sooner than we think, it's going to become obvious that to be anything other than our brothers' keepers endangers us all.[59]

Being Ready

As it happens, we're making the shift to dignitarian values in the nick of time. As the above list of possible setbacks suggests, the problems looming on the horizon are even tougher than those of the past, and solving them will require overcoming old divisions that block cooperation.

If we do discover life on other planets, we'll want to know where we stand relative to it on the evolutionary scale. If this analysis is correct, then dignitarianism is universal and it won't matter if extraterrestrial beings are more advanced than we because they will also be dignitarian and will protect our dignity much as we increasingly concern ourselves with the dignity of animals. And if it turns out that they are less advanced than we, then we will treat them with dignity. Either way, we should be okay—if, when that day comes, we've let go of our old predatory strategy in favor of a dignitarian one.

It's worth reminding ourselves that although we've been making models from the start, we've only become really good at it in the last few centuries. This suggests that we are probably much closer to the beginning of human history than the end.

It's myopic to believe that the problems we're confronting now are insoluble and will continue to obsess humans of the future. Even in the last hundred years, we've halved the percentage of people whose primary concern is food and shelter. Likewise, there are already signs that our focus is shifting from issues of war and peace, and domination and dignity, to global threats like those listed above. These will likely prove as bracing as those we've been focused on.

The apparent infinitude of our ignorance has an upside. In a perpetually unfolding reality, our business will remain unfinished, our understanding incomplete. This means that there will always be opportunities to contribute to knowledge. We, or our successors, will never be out of a job. As David Deutsch argues, we're at "the beginning of infinity."[60]

Einstein's Question: Is the Universe Friendly?

The eye with which I see God is the same eye with which God sees me.

– Meister Eckhart, 13th c. German mystic

Asked what question he would most want to know the answer to if he returned to Earth in 500 years, Albert Einstein replied, "Is the universe friendly?"

Through an open skylight over my bed, I can see the phases of the moon, the stars, an occasional plane, and, at dawn, soaring birds. A few sparrows have flown inside and found their way out again. Now and then a squirrel peeks over the edge. But apart from these locals, I do not feel seen as I peer into the cosmos.

Peering into its infinitude, I have no sense that the universe returns my gaze. Its eye is cold, if not blind. See someone seeing you and you exist. Look long enough into a fathomless void and you begin to ask, "Who am I? What am I doing here? Does anything matter?" My lifetime an instant, my body a speck, myself unremarked. At first glance, the universe seems uncaring; the indifference of infinite space, a cosmic indignity.

But then the old saying "God helps those who help themselves" pops into my head. And President Kennedy's variant thereof: "Here on Earth, God's work must truly be our own." If instead of gazing outward, we turn our attention inward, we discover that the universe does have a heart—indeed, lots of them. They're beating in our breasts.

Any inventory of the cosmos that omits us is like a survey of the body that overlooks the brain. In evolving the human mind, the universe has fashioned an instrument capable of understanding itself and empathizing with others. We are that instrument, and since we are part of the cosmos, we err if we judge it to lack kindness, love, and compassion. If I believe the universe is heartless, it's because I myself do not love.

But what if the impersonal forces that extinguished the dinosaurs should hurl a comet at us? There's a crucial difference between then and now. The demise of the dinosaurs made room for the appearance of mammals and thus for hominids. In the sixty-five million years since the dinosaurs vanished, there evolved a creature possessed of sophisticated modeling skills. If we use our talents wisely, they will enable us to avoid all manner of potential catastrophes—those of our own making as well as asteroids with our name on them.

The passage to a dignitarian world will probably not be smooth. We still have to lift billions of people out of poverty. Each year millions of children die from malnutrition and millions more suffer from malrecognition. But despair is unwarranted. The universe cares as much as we do. It has a heart—our very own. We are at once compassionate beings and modelers—the questing knights of Arthurian legend. In that eternal pursuit lies the imperishable dignity of humankind.

The universe, for its part, is likely to be as friendly or unfriendly as we are. Indeed, there is reason to hope.

ACKNOWLEDGEMENTS

My views on values, politics, and religion took shape during ten years of conversations with Peter A. Putnam (1926–1987), beginning in 1957 at Princeton University where we were both graduate students in physics. Although his private writings were voluminous, Putnam published only a few papers under his own name. He served as mentor to many, including myself.[61]

Both Putnam and I were privileged to experience a priceless apprenticeship with John A. Wheeler, who, as mentor to generations of physicists, generously shared his unique style of model-building with his students. Absent my apprenticeships with Putnam and Wheeler, this book would not exist.

I would also like to acknowledge valuable critiques provided by early readers of the manuscript, including Chuck Blitz, Robert Cabot, Ina Cooper, Adam Fuller, Charlotte Hill, David Hoffman, Tom Purvis, John Steiner, and Philip Turner.

The book also benefitted from comments made by readers of blogposts based on it and published at a variety of web sites.

At every stage of its development, Claire Sheridan critiqued and edited the manuscript. Her clarity, meticulous attention to detail, and encouragement were indispensable to the project.

Thanks also to Elisa Cooper for web site support, blogging assistance, and design of both the digital and print versions of this book.

When a book is mentioned in the text, but not footnoted, it is because it's listed among the Related Readings. Some of the material in this book draws upon prior ones: *Somebodies and Nobodies: Overcoming the Abuse of Rank* (New Society Publishers, 2003) and *All Rise: Somebodies, Nobodies, and the Politics of Dignity* (Berrett-Koehler, 2006).

ENDNOTES

1. From the PBS show, *The McLaughlin Group*, broadcast May 20, 2005.

2. *The God Delusion*, Richard Dawkins (Mariner Books, 2008); *The End of Faith*, Sam Harris (Norton, 2004); *God Is Not Great: How Religion Poisons Everything*, Christopher Hitchens (Warner Twelve, 2007).

3. Luke 2:14 (King James Version of *The New Testament*).

4. "The Imitation of Our Lord Don Quixote", Simon Leys, in *The New York Review of Books* (Vol. XLV, Number 10, pp. 32–35; June 11, 1998).

5. *The God Particle*, Leon Lederman and Dick Teresi (Mariner Books, 2006).

6. A semi-popular description of string theory can be found in *The Elegant Universe* by Brian Greene (New York: Vintage Paperback, 2000); and also in his *The Fabric of the Cosmos* (New York: Alfred A. Knopf, 2004).

7. *The New York Times*, August 26, 2005, p. C2.

8. For example, the discovery of seashells on mountaintops and fossil evidence of extinct species undermined theological doctrine that the world and all living things were a mere six thousand years old. Such discoveries posed a serious challenge to the Church's monopoly on truth.

9. Walter Truett Anderson discusses the evolving meaning of truth in his book *The Truth About the Truth: De-confusing and Re-constructing the Postmodern World* (New York: Tarcher, 1995).

10. If the past is a guide, we are unlikely ever to find a theory so comprehensive and accurate that it would bring an end to the search for more fundamental truths. Any model that accounted for all known phenomena would still be vulnerable to the possibility that new observations would reveal it to be incomplete. Recent developments suggest that in the same way that it can be shown that there are mathematical statements that are known to be true and yet are unprovable— Gödel's Theorem—it may be possible to show that there exist truths that no model could account for. See *Scientific American* (March 2009; pp. 19–20), *Impossible Inferences: A Mathematical Theory of Knowledge's Limits Takes Shape*, Graham P. Collins.

11. "The Unreasonable Effectiveness of Mathematics in the Natural Sciences", by E. P. Wigner, in *Communications in Pure and Applied Mathematics*, vol. 13, No. I (February 1960). New York: John Wiley & Sons.

12. From the Hymn by William Cowper (1731-1800).

13. Sometimes, closer examination reveals that what has been regarded as evidence is erroneous, and it is set aside.

14. See www.loyno.edu/twomey/blueprint/GoldenRule.jpg and religioustolerance.org/reciproc.htm.

15. See article by Domenico Parisi "Neminem laedere: Other-damaging behaviours and how to contain them": http://www.openabm.org/node/2268.

16. "The Moral Arc of History", *CADMUS*, Vol.1, Issue 3 (October 2011).

17. *Dipsychus.*

18. This proposition was debated at New York University and broadcast on "Intelligence Squared" in January 2012. The audience awarded the victory to the team that argued against religion.

19. A front page story in *The New York Times* on June 21, 2005 reported that a school teacher in rural Asia was accused of serially raping the fourth and fifth grade girls in his class. His pupils had dared not protest the absolute authority traditionally held by teachers. The situation reminded me of the unquestioning esteem in which, at least until the recent sex abuse scandals in America, priests were typically held by their parishioners. As the NYT article put it, "Parents grant teachers carte blanche, even condoning beatings, while students are trained to honor and obey teachers, never challenge them." An expert on Chinese education is quoted as saying, "The absolute authority of teachers in schools is one of the reasons that teachers are so fearless in doing what they want."

20. "Nuclear Disaster in Japan Was Avoidable, Critics Contend", *The New York Times* (March 10, 2012).

21. Google indicates no clear author and several users of this telling phrase.

22. Even when both parties to a dispute agree to let the evidence settle the matter, there can be disagreement over what constitutes evidence. One party might insist that anything in the Bible is ipso facto evidence, whereas the other might insist on substantiating biblical assertions with accepted historical and scientific procedures. The only way to settle an impasse like this—aside from one side backing down—is to build a meta-model that reconciles antagonist's views on basic methodological issues. If this proves impossible, then the only dignity-preserving recourse is to agree to disagree.

23. Betsy Leondar-Wright, *Class Matters* (Gabriola Island, B.C.: New Society Publishers, 2005). See p. 140.

24. This draws on material that appears in one of the author's previous books, *All Rise: Somebodies, Nobodies, and the Politics of Dignity* (Berrett-Koehler, 2006).

25. For example, Jean Klein, Nisargadatta, Wei Wu Wei, Douglas Harding, Hubert Benoit (and the commentary on his work by John H. G. Pierson), John Levy, Erwin Schrödinger, Thomas Merton, Martin Buber, Walter Truett Anderson, Chögyam Trungpa, Ram Dass, Franklin Merritt-Wolff, Atmananda, Joel Kramer, Robert Powell, Alan Watts, Heinrich Zimmer, Ramana Maharshi, Lao-tzu, Mo-tzu. The list goes on.

26. For example: *The Divine Comedy, Don Quixote, Paradise Lost, Faust, Moby Dick, The Brothers Karamazov,* and *Les Misérables.*

27. George Lemaître is known as the father of modern cosmology because he was the first person to solve Einstein's equations of gravitation as applied to the universe as a whole and to realize that Einstein's theory implied the Big Bang and cosmic expansion.

28. *The Day Without Yesterday: Lemaître, Einstein, and the Birth of Modern Cosmology,* John Farrell, pp. 24–25. (Thunder's Mouth Press, 2005). This book contains an incisive quote by the priest Father P. Ernest Verreux: "If there is a connection [between the Bible and science], it's a coincidence, and of no importance. And if you should prove to me that [a connection] exists, I would consider it unfortunate. It will merely encourage…people to imagine that the Bible teaches infallible science, whereas the most we can say is that occasionally one of the prophets made a correct scientific guess."

29. Op-ed page of *The New York Times*, November 12, 2005.

30. When the U.S.S.R. based its agricultural policy on a theory congruent with communist ideology, the result was widespread shortfalls in production. Cf. endnote 34.

31. Sankara, early 8th century Indian philosopher of Advaita Vedanta.

32. *The Better Angels of Our Nature: Why Violence Has Declined*, Steven Pinker (Viking, 2011).

33. *Report of the Program on Public Values*, Trinity College, Hartford, CN, (March, 2009).

34. During the Stalin years, the Soviet Union based agricultural policy on a rival theory—associated with the name of Trofim Lysenko—that supported communist ideology. The result was a calamitous setback for biology and agriculture in the USSR. Lysenko's theory harkened back to Lamarck's theory of acquired characteristics, which Darwin's had supplanted.

35. *The Mismeasure of Man*, Stephen Jay Gould (Norton, 1996).

36. Stephanie Coontz, *Marriage, a History: From Obedience to Intimacy or How Love Conquered Marriage* (New York: Viking, 2005).

37. The argument is made in full in "The Moral Arc of History", *CADMUS*, Vol.1, Issue 3 (October 2011).

38. It should not be overlooked that the current exception to the right to vote—people below the age of 18 in most countries—is incompatible with the principle of equal dignity for all, and would have to be rectified in a dignitarian society worthy of the name.

39. Steven LeBlanc and Katherine E. Register, *op cit.*

40. Mandelbrot is the mathematician who invented, and named, fractals.

41. More examples and discussion of rankism can be found in the author's book *Somebodies and Nobodies: Overcoming the Abuse of Rank* (New Society Publishers, 2003, 2004).

42. Betty Friedan, *The Feminine Mystique* (New York: Norton, 1963).

43. The coinage "sexism" is attributed to journalist and feminist Ellen Willis (1941–2006).

44. *Childism: Confronting Prejudice Against Children*, by Elisabeth Young-Bruehl (Yale University Press, 2012).

45. Speciesism is the name given to the belief that the rights of *Homo sapiens* take precedence of those of other species. In other words, human beings need not take into account the dignity of other species.

46. John Keats, *Ode on a Grecian Urn*.

47. *Why Beauty is Truth: A History of Symmetry* by Ian Stewart (New York: Basic Books, 2007).

48. Unless, of course, you are at the very bottom. But even then, you can resort to kicking the dog. Much cruelty to animals is a result of indignation that humans feel toward other humans who have humiliated them, but whom they dare not confront because the abusers are shielded by rank.

49. Whenever a "survival of the fittest" argument is invoked, a question of circularity arises: Can "fittest" be defined independently of "what survives"? In this case, the question takes the form: Can "dignitarian" be defined independently of "what prevails"? If not, the argument is circular, a mere tautology and it can tell us nothing about the curvature of the moral universe. Indeed, Darwin's theory was initially attacked as circular. Critics maintained that the only way we could gauge fitness was to look and see what survived.

Fortunately for the theory of natural selection, it is possible to state independent conditions that give organisms an advantage, or handicap them, in the struggle to survive and reproduce. Similarly, there is by now a long list of practices that are known to undermine dignity. The deselection of rankist organizations that tolerate rankism is analogous to the deselection of relatively unfit organisms in the struggle for reproductive survival. Darwin's principle is not circular (fitness criteria can be delineated independently of survivability), and since it can be foreseen that the inefficiencies attendant to rankism handicap organizations burdened by them, the notion that rankist values are recessive—and dignitarian values dominant—is not circular either.

50. *God's Politics*, Jim Wallis (HarperSanFrancisco, 2005).

51. In one party states, the Left/Right division occurs within the single ruling party.

52. George Lakoff, *Moral Politics: What Conservatives Know that Liberals Don't* (University of Chicago Press, 1996).

53. Or, as William Blake put it in *The Marriage of Heaven and Hell*, "You never know what is enough unless you know what is more than enough."

54. Philosophers such as John Rawls, Michael Walzer, and Avishai Margalit. See the *Related Readings* for references to their works.

55. *The Whole Earth Catalog*, http://www.edge.org/3rd_culture/brand09/brand09_index.html.

56. Pierre Baldi, *The Shattered Self: The End of Natural Evolution*, p. 113 (MIT Press, 2001).

57. Ray Kurzweil, *The Singularity Is Near: When Humans Transcend Biology* (New York: Viking, 2005). See also, Joel

Garreau, *Radical Evolution: The Promise and Peril of Enhancing
Our Minds, Our Bodies—And What It Means To Be Human*
(New York: Doubleday, 2005).

58. Matthew 5:44.

59. Genesis 4:9.

60. *The Beginning of Infinity*, David Deutsch (Viking, 2011)

61. In 1967, Wesleyan University Press published a talk I
gave on Putnam's work, titled "Causal and Moral Law—Their
Relationship as Examined in Terms of a Model of the Brain."
(Number 13 in a series of *Monday Evening Papers* presented at
Wesleyan University's Center for Advanced Study.) A related
paper, co-authored with Peter Putnam, which outlines his
Darwinian model of brain function, is titled "On the Origin
of Order in Behavior," and can be found in *General Systems*,
Vol. XI, pp. 99–112 (1966), Mental Health Research Institute,
University of Michigan, Ann Arbor, Michigan. I presented
Putnam's model at a number of universities, including
Columbia and Harvard Universities, The University of Texas
(Austin), Ohio State, Penn State, The University of California
(Irvine), and The State University of New York (Stony Brook),
The University of Massachusetts (Amherst), Wesleyan
University, and Battelle Memorial Institute in Columbus, OH.
A web site devoted to his work is www.peterputnam.org.

Related Readings

Acemoglu, Daron and Robinson, James A. *Why Nations Fail: The Origins of Power, Prosperity, and Poverty* (Crown Business, 2012)

Axelrod, Robert. *The Evolution of Cooperation*, Robert Axelrod (Basic Books, 1984)

Basu, K. and Kanbur, R., Editors. *Arguments for a Better World* (Oxford University Press, 2 Volumes, 2009)

Becker, Carl L. *The Heavenly City of the Eighteenth-Century Philosophers* (Yale University Press, 1932)

Brzezinski, Zbnigniew. *Second Chance: Three Presidents and the Crisis of American Superpower* (Basic Books, 2007)

Buchan, James. *The Authentic Adam Smith: His Life and Ideas* (W. W. Norton, 2006)

Christian, Brian. *The Most Human Human* (Doubleday, 2011)

Churchand, Patricia S. *Braintrust: What Neuroscience Tells Us about Morality* (Princeton University Press, 2011)

Colinvaux, Paul. *The Fates of Nations: A Biological Theory of History* (Simon and Shuster, 1980)

Corning, Peter. *The Fair Society: The Science of Human Nature and the Pursuit of Social Justice* (University of Chicago Press, 2011)

Cornwell, Paul. *Only by Failure: The Many Faces of the Impossible Life of Terence Gray* (Salt Publishing, Cambridge, U.K., 2004)

Dawkins, Richard. *The God Delusion* (Mariner Books, 2008)

de Botton, Alain. *Religion for Atheists: A Non-believer's Guide to the Uses of Religion* (Pantheon, 2012)

De Waal, Frans. *Primates and Philosophers: How Morality Evolves* (Princeton University Press, 2006)

DeLong, Howard. *Courts of Common Reason: Awakening the Spirit of 1776 to Form a More Perfect Union* (2nd Ed, 2011)

Dennett, Daniel. *Darwin's Dangerous Idea: Evolution and the Meanings of Life* (Simon & Schuster, 1995)

Douthat, Ross. *Bad Religion: How We Became a Nation of Heretics* (Free Press, 2012)

Eagleman, David. *Incognito: The Secret Lives of the Brain* (Vintage, 2011)

Frank, Adam. *The Constant Fire: Beyond the Science vs. Religion Debate* (University of California Press, 2010)

Friedel, Robert. *A Culture of Improvement: Technology and the Western Millennium* (MIT Press, 2007)

Fukuyama, Francis. *The End of History and the Last Man* (Free Press, 1996) and *The Origins of Political Order* (FSG, 2012)

Haidt, Jonathan. *The Righteous Mind: Why Good People Are Divided by Politics and Religion* (Pantheon, 2012)

Harding, Donald E. *Religions of the World: A Handbook for the Open-Minded* (First published in 1966. Reprinted by the Sholland Trust, 2007)

Harris, Sam. *The End of Faith* (Norton, 2004) and *The Moral Landscape* (Free Press, 2011) and *Free Will* (Free Press, 2012)

Hitchens, Christopher. *God Is Not Great: How Religion Poisons Everything* (Warner Twelve, 2007)

Hunt, Lynn. *Inventing Human Rights* (published in 2008 in connection with the British Museum's exhibit "Taking Liberties")

Jamieson, Dale. *Morality's Progress: Essays on Humans, Other Animals, and the Rest of Nature* (Oxford University Press, 2002)

Johnson, Allan G. *Privilege, Power, and Difference* (McGraw Hill, 2nd Ed. 2006)

Kateb, George. *Human Dignity* (Belknap Press, 2011)

Kurzban, Robert. *Why Everyone (Else) Is a Hypocrite: Evolution and the Modular Mind* (Princeton University Press, 2012)

LeBlanc, Steven A. and Register, Katherine E. *Constant Battles: The Myth of the Peaceful Nobel Savage* (St. Martin's Press, 2003)

Luhrmann, T.M. *When God Talks Back: Understanding the American Evangelical Relationship With God* (Knopf, 2012)

Margalit, Avishai. *The Decent Society* (Harvard University Press, 1996)

Oerter, Robert. *The Theory of Almost Everything* (Pi Press, 2006)

Ohanian, Hans C. *Einstein's Mistakes: The Human Failings of Genius* (Norton, 2008)

Plantinga, Alvin. *Where Conflict Really Lies: Science, Religion, & Naturalism* (Oxford University Press, 2012)

Potter, Stephen. *One-upmanship* (Moyer Bell, 2005)

Potts, Malcolm and Hayden, Thomas. *Sex and War: How Biology Explains Warfare and Terrorism and Offers a Path to a Safer Future* (Ben Bella Books, 2008)

Rawls, John. *A Theory of Justice* (Belknap Press, 1999)

Ridley, Matt. *Origin of Virtue* (Penguin, 1998)

Rosen, Michael. *Dignity: Its History and Meaning* (Harvard University Press, 2012)

Schmookler, Andrew Bard. *The Parable of the Tribes: The Problem of Power in Social Evolution* (University of California Press, 1984)

Shermer, Michael. *Science of Good and Evil* (Holt, 2004)

Shipler, David. *The Working Poor: Invisible in America* (Vintage, 2005)

Shorto, Russell. *Descartes' Bones: A Skeletal History of the Conflict Between Faith and Reason* (Doubleday, 2008)

Shumaker, Robert W.; Walkup, Kristina R.; Beck, Benjamin B. *Animal Tool Behavior* (Johns Hopkins Press, 2011)

Smil, Vaclav. *Global Catastrophes and Trends: The Next Fifty Years* (The MIT Press, 2008)

Smith, Adam. *The Theory of Moral Sentiments* (Oxford University Press, 1976)

Taves, Ann. *Religious Experience Reconsidered* (Princeton University Press: 2010)

Tiedemann, Paul. *Human Dignity as Legal Concept. A Philosophical Clarification* (See www.dr-tiedemann.de/buch07eng.htm)

Walzer, Michael. *Spheres of Justice* (Basic Books, 1983)

ABOUT THE AUTHOR

Robert W. Fuller earned his Ph.D. in physics at Princeton University and taught at Columbia, where he co-authored *Mathematics of Classical and Quantum Physics*. He then served as president of Oberlin College, his alma mater. For a dozen years, beginning in 1978, he worked in what came to be known as "citizen diplomacy" to improve the Cold War relationship. During the 1990s, he served as board chair of the non-profit global corporation Internews, which promotes democracy via free and independent media. In 2004 he was elected a Fellow of the World Academy of Art and Science, and in 2011 he served as keynote speaker at the National Conference on Dignity for All hosted by the president of Bangladesh.

With the end of the Cold War and the collapse of the USSR, Fuller looked back on his career and understood that he had been, at different times in his life, a somebody and a nobody. His periodic sojourns into "Nobodyland" led him to identify and probe rankism—abuse of the power inherent in rank—and ultimately to write *Somebodies and Nobodies: Overcoming the Abuse of Rank* (New Society Publishers, 2003). Three years later, he published a sequel focusing on building a "dignitarian" society, titled *All Rise: Somebodies, Nobodies, and the Politics of Dignity* (Berrett-Koehler, 2006). An Indian edition was published in 2007 (Viveka Foundation), a Chinese trnslation in 2008, and a Bengali translation in 2009. Fuller has also co-authored (with Pamela A. Gerloff) a short practical guide for creating dignity in our homes, schools, workplaces, and the world titled *Dignity for All: How to Create a World without Rankism* (June 2008, Berrett-Koehler Publishers).

Connect with Robert W. Fuller Online

Web site: www.robertworksfuller.com

Facebook: www.facebook.com/robertwfuller

Twitter: twitter.com/#!/robertwfuller

Made in the USA
Charleston, SC
30 September 2012